Antonio Aruta Improta

Regulations on the prevention and remediation of environmental damage: a comparison between Directive 2004/35/EC and Legislative Decree 152/2006

Title | Regulations on the prevention and remediation of environmental damage: a comparison between Directive 2004/35/EC and Legislative Decree 152/2006
Author | Antonio Aruta Improta
ISBN | 978-88-31624-63-3

Youcanprint
Via Marco Biagi 6 - 73100 Lecce
www.youcanprint.it
info@youcanprint.it

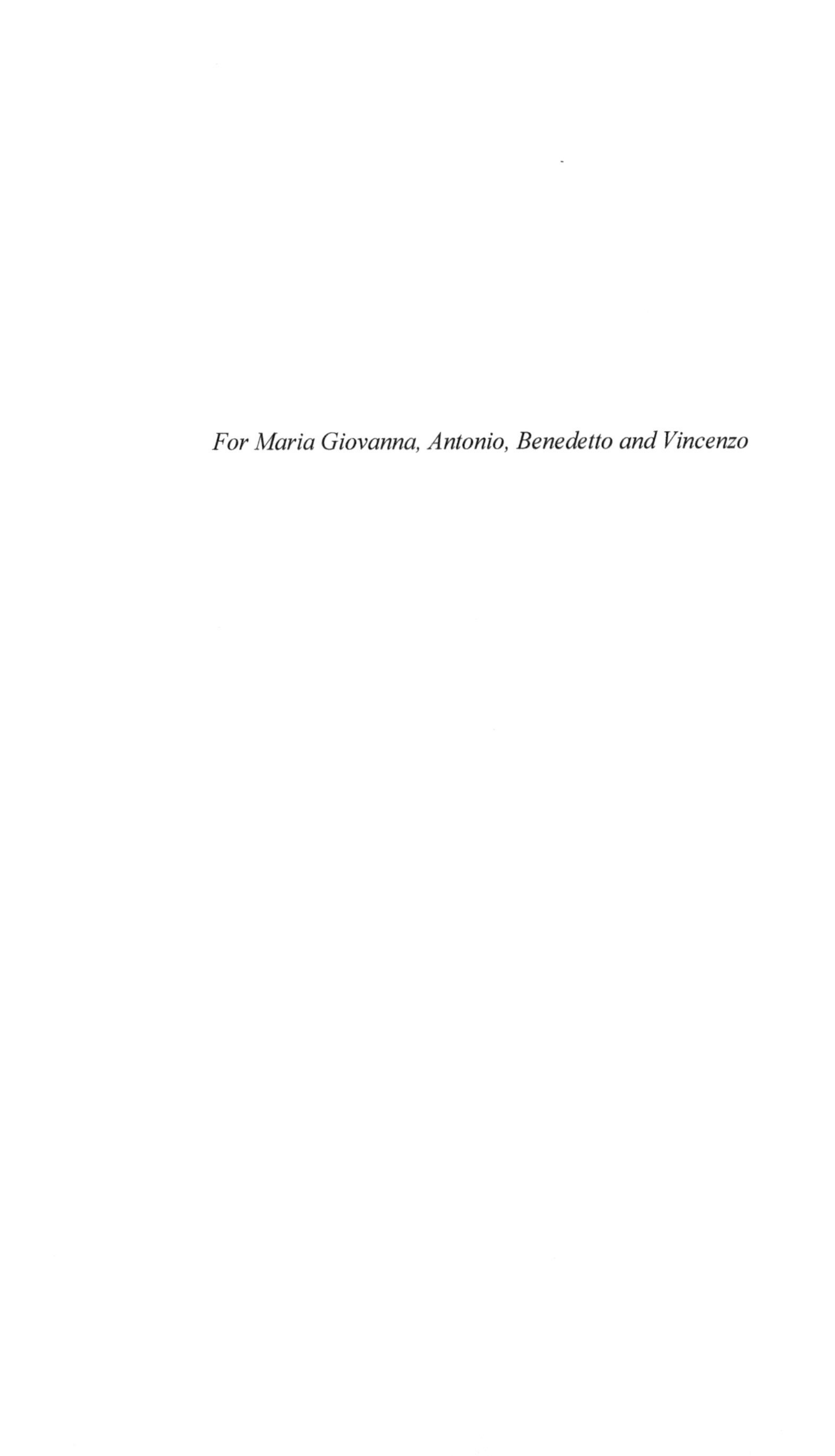

For Maria Giovanna, Antonio, Benedetto and Vincenzo

Table of Contents

Introduction

Regulations on the prevention and remediation of environmental damage are some of the most sensitive and controversial legal instruments.

In response to the growing problems affecting the global ecosystem, many disputes are raised about the causal contribution of Man in causing these problems and on the efficiency of approved regulations to prevent and remedy the impairment caused to environmental media.

The main impediment of an effective action against environmental problems is in fact specifically determined by the lack of a systematic and precise nature in environmental legislation.

This is especially seen in international law, characterized, on one hand, by the production of legal deeds that contain general rules but no binding efficacy by their nature, i.e. statements of principles; on the other, by the production of various binding regulations such as treaties, albeit only sectorial ones. Examples of this are the "International Convention for the Prevention of Pollution from Ships" on hydrocarbons, and the recently approved "Paris Agreement" on Climate.

Moreover, rather than giving a comprehensive legal classification of environmental damage *per se*, international regulations only establish a general prohibition for cross-border pollution. The supranational system, in fact, allows states to arbitrarily exploit their resources in principle, provided this does not cause damage to the territory of other States, quantifiable in terms of losses suffered by people, damage to property, cleaning costs and other impairments deriving from pollution.

In various instances, the claim of the aforementioned laws has actually been detrimental to the global environment, for both economic and political reasons, without causing any consequences to the liable States.

Evidence of this is the accident of April 26th, 1986 at the nuclear power plant in Chernobyl. The widespread environmental disaster caused by this catastrophe did not generate repercussions at a judicial level neither for the State of origin of the power plant, Ukraine, then belonging to the hegemonic Soviet Union, nor to the nuclear lobby, very influential in the political and economic life of the country. The accident, therefore, is among the major cases of impunity in history.

This also holds true for the uncontrolled development of some Nations that are currently considered superpowers, so advanced at an industrial and productive level that they have created serious problems of cross-border atmospheric pollution, these problems were not addressed by the judicial authorities.

It is enough to think of China's exponential growth in the past few years, determined by a total lack, until recently, of environmental and labor legislation, as well as by the indifference of other States to the serious repercussions that such arbitrary development has generated on the global environment.

Based on these considerations, European institutions have rightly endorsed a common legislation for all EU Member States, namely the Directive 2004/35/EC on environmental liability, with regard to the prevention and remedying of environmental damage.

Unlike international sector agreements, the European Directive legally identifies environmental damage, imposing the implementation of preventative measures in situations where a threat of environmental damage is present. It also imposes to concretely repair the natural resources and/or damaged services.

The burden of undertaking such measures is placed on the operator responsible for the damage or for the threat of such damage, being the only subject to be held liable on the basis of the restrictive interpretation of the "polluter pays" principle, which forms the basis of the environmental liability regulation.

Although the framework directive allows the approval of stricter national laws, as a rule, the aforementioned liability from which prevention and remedy obligations arise is not attributed, even jointly, to the State from whose territory the damage to natural resources was caused.

This circumstance can obviously undermine the remedy of the damaged natural media themselves, since the State or the competent authority not required to undertake preventative and remedial actions in the cases in which the responsible operator cannot be identified, or if he is unable to bear the costs of the aforementioned actions. Moreover, with particular regard to the latter case, the directive suggests -but does not impose- insurance coverage for the environmental damage caused by the operators, even if they carry out professional activities considered by the legislation itself as potentially dangerous to health and the environment.

In Italy's domestic law, many questionable provisions exist concerning the special regulation on environmental liability as set out in Articles 298 bis-318, Part Six, of Legislative Decree no. 152 of 2006, also known as the Environmental Code or the Consolidated Environmental Law, which implemented Directive 2004/ 35 / EC.

Various provisions appear to be conceptually confusing, not coordinated between each other and non-compliant with the provisions of the European Framework Directive, especially regarding the environmental liability system and the criteria for assessing the damage to natural resources.

Therefore, the purpose of this paper is to reconstruct, in the clearest and most comprehensible way possible, the fragmented scenario of the legislation on compensation for environmental damage, as defined in the twenty articles of the sixth part of the Environmental code, comparing them to the contents of the European Directive and indicating its critical points, offering points for reflection.

The paper, in particular, analyzes the evolution of the concept of "environment" and of the controversial notion of environmental damage as a multi-factor offense. In this regard, the negative repercussions that ecological damage can cause to the individual sphere of the various subjects are pointed out, whether these are physical or juridical persons who, therefore, can act independently in court for the compensation of the damages suffered. Such damages can also have a material nature, impacting the quality of life of the person who suffers the consequences of the environmental media's contamination.

The analysis of the environmental liability system then follows, as well as the compensation and quantification of damages caused only to natural resources.

Evaluation criteria were used, whose purpose was to allow a real and specific remedy of the environmental media and/or of their compromised services.

Lastly, attention was devoted to some particular cases of environmental liability that have been the subject of debate in case-law and literature: the several liability of polluters and of the owner or manager of the damaged site.

Chapter 1

LEGAL NATURE OF THE ENVIRONMENTAL DAMAGE

1.1. The environment, a material asset

Within the Italian legal system, the technical-legal problems of the legislation on compensation for environmental damages mentioned in the introduction stem, first of all, from the complex definition of the legal asset protected by the legislation itself, namely the environment.

To date, in fact, there have been heated debates both in case-law and literature on the classification of the aforementioned asset.

As a preliminary point, it can be stated that the etymology of the Italian word "ambiente" (environment), which derives from the Latin word *ambiens-entis*, expresses the idea of being around, of surrounding. Thus, the meaning of the word "environment" is that of a «set of conditions external to the organism where plant and animal life takes place» or in a figurative sense, a «set of external materials, social and cultural conditions in which a human being develops, lives and works».[1] The various theories expressed by philosophers, theologians, scientists and economists have surely significantly influenced the gradual evolution of the legal system regarding the concept of "environment".

In fact, from the analysis of international and national sector regulations, there is an anthropocentric projection typical of the Greco-Roman period and mistakenly supported deduced from the common Christian vision of the Western world.[2] However, to be concise, the

---

[1] As reported under the word "Ambiente" (Environment) in the Dictionary of the Italian language Zanichelli, 11th edition.

[2] For a correct interpretation of the Christian vision of nature, refer to the considerations made by Pope Francis, *Laudato si'. Testo integrale dell'enciclica* (Full text of the Encyclical), edited by C. Simonelli, Piemme, 2015; See also P. Haffner, *Visione Cristiana dell'ambiente frutto della creazione di Dio* (Christian vision of the

confirmation of the theories referred to was omitted, and can be consulted directly for in-depth knowledge.[3]

At the international level, public interest in the environment was recognized in case-law in 1941, following the outcome of an arbitral dispute between Canada and the US due to air pollution caused by emissions from a Canadian foundry in Trail, located at a short distance from the border with the United States.

On that occasion, one of the fundamental environmental principles was stated, which soon became an international custom, according to which «no State has the right to use or allow its territory to be used in such a way as to cause damage».[4]

This principle established a ban on cross-border pollution, based on which Canada was ordered to compensate the damage to the US agriculture caused by the harmful emissions of sulfur dioxide from the industrial production processes of the Canadian foundry.

However, the first definition of "environment" was introduced into the international legal system with the subsequent UN Declaration at the Conference on Human Environment:[5] «The natural resources of the Earth, including air, water, land, flora and fauna, and particularly representative samples of natural ecosystems must be preserved, in the interest of present and future generations, through an adequate planning and management».[6]

Subsequently, the International Court of Justice drafted a concept of environment comprising, in addition to the «space where human beings

---

environment, fruit of God's creation), Gracewing, 2012.

[3] See A. Pottier, *Comment les économistes réchauffent la planète*, SEUIL, 2016; P. Descola, *L'ecologia degli altri. L'antropologia e la questione della natura* (The ecology of others. Anthropology and the question of nature), Linaria, 2013; D. Porena, *La protezione dell'ambiente tra Costituzione italiana e "Costituzione globale"* (The protection of the environment between the Italian Constitution and the "Global Constitution"), Giappichelli, Torino, 2009.

[4] See Arbitration Judgment of March 11, 1941, *UN Reports of International Arbitral Awards*, vol. III, 1941, page 1965.

[5] Held in Stockholm from 5 to 16 June 1972.

[6] Stockholm declaration, principle 2.

live», also the quality of life and the health of human beings, including future generations.[7]

The concept of environment was therefore reconstructed in a purely anthropocentric way, its protection mainly stemming from the need to ensure the well-being of present and future human generations.

In this regard, the principle of sustainable development was clearly expressed, defined for the first time by the Bruntdland report, understood as «development that meets the needs of the present without compromising the ability of future generations to meet their own needs».[8]

This was also clearly expressed in the first principle of the 1992 Rio de Janeiro Declaration on Environment and Development,[9] according to which «human beings are at the center of problems for sustainable development. They have the right to a healthy and productive life in harmony with nature».

In the legal documents drafted at the Community level, instead, the supremacy of man over nature tended to weaken.

In 1985, the European Community approved Council Directive no. 337/85 of 27 June 1985, concerning the environmental impact assessment of certain public and private projects, according to which the

---

[7] International Court of Justice, advisory opinion on the lawfulness of the use of nuclear weapons issued on 8 July 1996.

[8] The Brundtland report, also known as "The future of all of us" is a document issued in 1987 by the World Commission on Environment and Development (WCED) which introduced the concept of "sustainable development" for the first time. Regarding the principle being examined, please refer to the considerations made by J.D. Sachs, *L'era dello sviluppo sostenibile* (The Age of Sustainable development), in Frontiers, Bocconi Editore University, 2015; F. Salvia, *Ambiente e sviluppo sostenibile* (Environment and Sustainable Development), in Rivista Giuridica Ambiente, 1998; M. Politi, *Tutela dell'ambiente e «sviluppo sostenibile». Profili e prospettive di evoluzione nel diritto internazionale alla luce della Conferenza di Rio de Janeiro* (Environmental protection and «sustainable development». Profile and perspectives of evolution in international law in the light of the Conference of Rio de Janeiro), Padova, 1995.

[9] The Rio Declaration is one of the valuable documents produced by the Earth Summit, the first world conference on the environment, held from 3 to 14 June 1992, in which 172 governments and 2400 representatives of non-governmental organizations participated.

environment represents the following elements: «1) man, fauna and flora; 2) soil, water, air, climate and landscape; 3) material assets and cultural heritage; 4) the interaction between the elements referred to in the first, second and third point».[10]

A few years later, in the Council of Europe's Convention on Civil Liability for Damage Resulting from Activities Dangerous to the Environment,[11] it was stated that the notion of environment encompassed all the natural resources and the interactions between them, the assets forming part of the cultural heritage and the characteristic aspects of the landscape.[12]

Therefore, with respect to international regulations, European requirements provided for a fundamental element, represented by the concept of an "interrelation" between man and natural resources. This criterion marked the trend towards the ecological and less anthropic awareness that has been developing to date: being man interdependent with nature, he has the duty to necessarily protect the environment in which he lives.

It should be noted that the concept of ecology must be kept separate from that of environmentalism. "Ecology", [comp. of *eco* and *logia*, a word created (from the German Oekologie) by biologist E. Haeckel (1986)[13]], indeed, is not an ideal or a movement, but an interdisciplinary field that includes the biology and sciences of the Earth, focusing on the scientific analysis and study of the interactions between the organisms and their environment.

Therefore, the European institutions have devoted to the environment (strictly speaking) the entire Title XX of the Treaty on the Functioning of the European Union (TFEU),[14] namely, Articles. 191, 192 and 193,[15]

---

[10] Directive 1985/337/EEC, art. 3.

[11] Signed in Lugano in 1993.

[12] See the Lugano Convention on civil liability for damage to the environment resulting from dangerous activities, art. 2.10.

[13] As found under the entry "Ecologìa" in the Treccani dictionary.

[14] The Treaty on the Functioning of the European Union (TFEU) and the Treaty of the European Union (TEU), make up the Lisbon Treaty, signed in 2007 and entered into force on December 1, 2009.

[15] Pursuant to Articles 174, 175 and 176 of the Treaty establishing the European

within which the principles, criteria and objectives of the Union's environmental policy were stated.

Within the Italian legal system, instead, the definition of environment as a legal asset has found some initial complications at the constitutional level.

The notion of "environment" was in fact not explicitly mentioned in the text of the new Constitution of Italy, which became effective on 1 January 1948.[16] The founders limited themselves to providing for a generic "protection of the landscape", without giving further details on the meaning of the word.

Given this legal loophole, the Italian Supreme Court (*Corte di Cassazione*), through an interpretation of the combined provisions of Articles 2, 9 and 32 of the Constitution, which refer respectively to the recognition of the inviolable rights of man and to the protection of the landscape and health, has described the subjective right to a healthy environment.

From an anthropic point of view, constitutional relevance to the environment was indirectly recognized, as it is functional to the protection of certain fundamental interests of an individual.[17]

Subsequently, the first judgment of the Constitutional Court on environmental matters identified -in the provisions of art. 9, paragraph 2, of the Constitution-, the legislative reference implicit in the naturalistic value of the assets forming the Nation's landscape as well as its cultural and artistic heritage.

In this regard, the landscape, mentioned as one of the fundamental

---

Community (TEC). The latter document was renamed after the entry into force of the Treaty of Maastricht, signed in 1992 and entered into force in 1993. Originally, in fact, it was named the Treaty establishing the European Economic Community (TEEC), signed in Rome in 1957.

[16] The Constitution of the Italian Republic is the Fundamental Law of Italy, approved by the Constituent Assembly on December 22, 1947 and entered into force on January 1, 1948. In the *Gazzetta Ufficiale* no. 298, extraordinary edition of December 27, 1947.

[17] See *Corte di Cassazione*, verdict no. 5172 of 1979. On this point, see T. Montanari, *Unfinished Constitution. Art, landscape, environment*, Einaudi, 2013; F. Lucarelli, *Environment, territory and cultural heritage in the constitutional jurisprudence*, Italian Scientific Editions, 2006; S. Patti, *Constitutional values and environmental protection*, in G. Alpa, M. Alberighi, *Law and Environment. Materials of doctrine and jurisprudence*, Padua 1984.

principles of the Constitution, was defined as «a primary, aesthetic and cultural value».[18]

Moreover, although Law no. 349 of 8 July 1986 had established the Ministry of the Environment and issued the first provisions regarding an environmental damage, it did not provide an exhaustive definition of the environment, limiting itself to protecting it in its unity.[19] The definition is also missing in the Legislative Decree no. 152 dated April 3rd, 2006, known as the Environmental Code.[20]

Nevertheless, the aforesaid unified vision of the environment as an asset determined the gradual transition from a "set" of elements to a "system", supporting the interrelations between the various elements that compose it.

A subsequent ruling by the Constitutional Court, in fact, defined the environment as a «fundamental right of the human being and a fundamental interest of the community», affirming a unitary notion of the environment as an asset, that included all natural and cultural resources. In particular, it was clarified that the environment includes

The conservation, rational management and improvement of natural conditions (air, water, soil and territory in all its components), the existence and preservation of the terrestrial and marine genetic heritage of all the animal and plant species that live in it, in a natural state, and ultimately, the human being in all its expressions.[21]

Later, another judgment of the Court radically contradicted the definition of "environment" as a "complex of material things" contained in the previous one. Such judgment described the environment as a unitary, intangible asset «however made of various components, each of which could also constitute, separately and individually, an object of care and protection; but all of them, as a whole, could be traced back to a unity». Nevertheless, it was also stated that although the environment

---

[18] Constitutional Court, judgment no. 151 of 1986.
[19] See Law no. 349 of 1986, art. 1 and 18.
[20] Published in the *Gazzetta Ufficiale* (Official Journal) no. 88 of 14 April 2006.
[21] Constitutional Court, judgment no. 210 of 1987.

was protected as an incisive element on the quality of life, it could not have been the subject of individual actions of an appropriative type, highlighting the legal nature of the interest in environmental protection as a "widespread interest". The environment, therefore, took on a primary and absolute value. Its protection was based on articles 2, 9 and 32 of the Constitution, and on ordinary laws which, in compliance with these regulations, governed and guaranteed the enjoyment of the asset while also ensuring its protection, even by imposing specific obligations of supervision and actions to be taken.[22]

Lastly, a subsequent ruling re-affirmed the concept according to which the environment is «a unitary asset, even if it is composed of many relevant aspects for the natural and human life».[23]

In this regard, the Italian Supreme Court (*Corte di Cassazione*) has specified that damage to the environment, as an immaterial but legally recognized and protected asset in its unity, must be kept separate from damage caused to its individual components: the structure of the territory, the wealth of its natural resources, the landscape in its aesthetic and cultural value and the condition of a healthy life. Moreover, even if the State, as the supreme authority of the national community, centralizes the entitlement to compensation for damage to the environment on itself, this does not preclude the possibility for other individuals to claim the protection of other personal or property rights harmed by damage to the environment in court, such as, for example, damage to the right to health.[24]

It should be noted that the aforementioned case-law contribution of the Supreme Court (*Corte di Cassazione*) has become necessary since the previous article 18 of Law 349/198,[25] defined based on article 2043 of the Civil Code, which provided for damage compensation due to an illicit event, explicitly allowed to remedy "generic" environmental damage solely for the benefit of the State.

---

[22] Constitutional Court, judgment n. 641 of 1987.

[23] Constitutional Court, judgment no. 1029 of 1988.

[24] See Italian Supreme Court (*Corte di Cassazione*), judgment no. 440 of 1989.

[25] Repealed by art. 318. 2, lett. a) of the Environmental Code, with the exception of paragraph v.

Moreover, the Supreme Court (*Corte di Cassazione*) established that "environment" in a juridical sense meant a "set" which -although including various material assets- differed ontologically from these, since it identified itself with an immaterial reality that was the expression of an autonomous collective value, that, as such, was specifically the object of protection by the legal system through law no. 349 of 1986. Therefore, the damage caused to the environment through harm to one of the elements that compose it (air, water, earth, etc.), has an independent importance with respect to the damage caused to its individual components.[26]

The environment, therefore, was initially intended as a set of material things, as a fundamental right of the person and a fundamental interest of the community (public property with a public function). Later, however, the environment was more correctly defined as a unitary intangible asset, of widespread interest, as well as a primary and absolute value, albeit remaining limited to the constitutionally guaranteed subjective rights in its meaning of being the right to a healthy environment.

The subsequent Constitutional Law no. 3 of 2001[27] introduced for the first time the concept of «protection of the environment, of the ecosystem and of cultural heritage» under the State's exclusive legislative competence, in art. 117 of the Constitution, also including the «valorization of cultural and environmental heritage» under the Regional authorities' competence.

However, this purely formal act by the Parliament generated doubts about the meaning of the definitions mentioned in quotes and about the enforcement of the responsibilities themselves.[28]

Faced with this legislative inaccuracy and based on the aforementioned judgments, the case-law continued to conceive the environment as a subject only in a non-technical way, pursuant to art. 117 of the Constitution, as it was aimed at defining a value, however

---

[26] See *Corte di Cassazione*, judgment no. 4362 of 1992.

[27] Laying down "Amendments to Title V of Part Two of the Constitution", published in the *Gazzetta Ufficiale* (Official Journal) no. 248 of October 24th, 2001.

[28] See B. Pozzo, M. Renna, *L'ambiente nel nuovo titolo V della Costituzione* (The environment in the new Title V of the Constitution), Giuffrè, 2004.

cross-referenced, insofar as it was functional to the protection of other constitutionally guaranteed assets and rights.

The State was therefore responsible for the environmental policies and for setting the minimum environmental protection standards. The Regional authorities were instead responsible for the environment's enhancement, i.e. the right to improve and tighten up the standards (so-called *"derogation in melius"*), based on the fact they were able to directly legislate on the protection of the environment on a residual basis by applying the European subsidiarity and integration principles.[29]

In particular, based on the principle of subsidiarity,[30] pursuant to art. 118 of the Constitution, «The State, Regions, Provinces, Metropolitan City of Rome Capital authorities and Municipalities favored the initiative of citizens, individually or in association, to carry out activities of general interest».

This principle could be interpreted, on the one hand, as a vertical distribution of administrative allocations from the central body, i.e. the State, towards the local public bodies closer to the citizens and to the territory's priorities (so-called vertical subsidiarity); on the other, as a possibility for the citizens, individually or in association, to assist the institutions with regard to the measures affecting the situations that strictly concern them (so-called horizontal subsidiarity).

---

[29] See Constitutional Court (*Corte Costituzionale*), judgment no. 108 of 2005; no. 307 of 2003; no. 407 of 2002.

[30] The subsidiarity principle has been endorsed at the European level in order to regulate the separation of powers between the EU and member countries in all shared subjects, including the environment. In fact, although the first is recognized - in conjunction with art. 5.3 of the Treaty on European Union (TEU) and of art. 4.2, lett. e) of the Treaty on the Functioning of the European Union (TFEU) - own competences related to environmental protection, that would not result in exclusive competence, since the second is in fact able to legislate on environmental matters. On the principle under consideration, reference is made to the considerations of B. Di Giacomo Russo, *Il valore della sussidiarietà. Origini e attualità.* (The value of subsidiarity. Origins and current events), in Doctrine and institutions, Città Nuova, 2015; C. Zilioli, *L'applicazione del principio di sussidiarietà nel diritto comunitario dell'ambiente.* (The application of the principle of subsidiarity in community environmental law), in Rivista Giuridica Ambiente, 1995.

The principle of integration instead states that: «Environmental protection needs must be integrated into the definition and implementation of EU policies and actions, in particular with a view to promoting sustainable development».[31]

The aim of this latter principle, therefore, is to ensure that the policies and measures promoted by the European Union or the Member States are adequately assessed based on the aspects concerning a necessary environmental protection.

With judgment no. 196 of 2004, the Constitutional Court (*Corte Costituzionale*), stated *inter alia* that the landscape, as a «form of territory and environment», has repeatedly been understood as a primary constitutional value, in the sense of its «insusceptibility of subordination to any other constitutionally protected value, including economic ones».

On the other hand, the Court added that «this does not legitimize an absolute primacy in a hypothetical hierarchical scale of constitutional values, rather it creates the necessity for them to always be taken into account in the actual balancing implemented by ordinary legislators and public administrations».

With judgments no. 367 and 378 of 2007, however, the case-law orientation of the Court once again conceived the environment as a tangible asset specifically susceptible to protection, meaning, an actual, technical matter of exclusive competence of the State.

The Regions (Regional Authorities) always have the possibility of improving the national minimum environmental standards indirectly and in a mediated way, legislating on the subjects of their competence related to the environment (health, civil protection, etc.), therefore applying only the principle of integration.

It seems clear that the aforementioned opinions issued by the Constitutional Court (*Corte Costituzionale*) have caused a legitimate

---

[31] Maastricht Treaty on the European Union, art. 6, then art. 11 of the *Trattato sul funzionamento dell'Unione Europea* (Treaty on the Functioning of the European Union). On the principle of integration, see M. Cartabia, N. Lupo, A. Simoncini, *Democracy and subsidiarity in the EU. National Parliaments, regions and civil society in the decision-making process*, in Percorsi, il Mulino, 2013.

perplexity. Either the environment is a subject only in a non-technical way, maintaining the exploitation of environmental assets, with the Regions authorized to make laws directly on the environment to improve national standards; or the environment is a subject on its own, of exclusive State competence, with the Regions only able to legislate by proxy, pursuant to art. 117 of the Constitution.[32]

Therefore, for reasons of certainty regarding the application of the constitutional provision in question, it would be more correct to reconsider the environment merely as a transversal value, adding it, among others, to the new constitutionally relevant "rights-duties", by virtue of the combined provisions of art. 2 and 54 of the Constitution.

Article 2 of the Constitution (Charter of Fundamental Rights), which recognizes and generically guarantees the inviolable rights of man, is considered a so-called "open norm", suitable to give a constitutional coverage to other fundamental rights not explicitly mentioned in the text of the Constitution, which were however recognized over time within the Italian legal system.

Thanks to the aforementioned provision, in combination with articles 9 and 32 of the Constitution, the literature has in fact hermeneutically elaborated the fundamental right of an individual to environmental healthiness.

Moreover, the provision of paragraph II of art. 2 of the Constitution, which refers to the obligations of political, economic and social solidarity, allows those interpreting it to consider the environment also as the obligation of an individual man and of the institutions within which he carries out his personality.[33]

---

[32] Of this opinion, see M. Cecchetti, *La materia "tutela dell'ambiente e dell'ecosistema" nella giurisprudenza costituzionale: lo stato dell'arte e i nodi ancora irrisolti* (The subject "protection of the environment and the ecosystem" in constitutional literature: the state of art and still unresolved issues), in federalismi.it, issue number 7 - 08/04/2009. For an in-depth analysis of the topic, see S. Grassi, *Problemi di diritto costituzionale dell'ambiente* (Problems of Constitutional Law of the Environment), Milano, 2012; M. Cecchetti, *Principi costituzionali per la tutela dell'ambiente* (Constitutional principles for environmental protection), Milano, 2000.
[33] According to art. 2 of the Constitution «the Republic recognizes and guarantees the

The parallel obligation of protection and of political solidarity in environmental matters in particular, though not yet explicitly recognized, originates from the European Environmental Policy that the Italian State has undertaken to observe and implement by joining the legal system of the European Union.[34]

Italy's entry into the EU took place pursuant to art. 2, paragraph II, of the Constitution, according to which Italy «consents to limit its sovereignty, in a position of equality with other States, in favor of a system that guarantees peace and justice among nations; it promotes and favors international organizations with this purpose».

In addition to art. 2 of the Constitution, art. 54 of the Constitution was also applied, stating that «all citizens have the obligation to be loyal to the Republic and to observe its Constitution and laws».

On this subject, the Brazilian Constitution merits to be mentioned, which in art. 225, Chapter VI, establishes a precise right-obligation for both the public authority and the community: «Everyone has the right to an ecologically balanced environment, an asset for common use by the people, and essential to the wholesome healthy quality of life; this imposes upon the public authorities and community the obligation to defend and preserve it for present and future generations».

In our legal system, therefore, only by considering the environment as a subjective right and a constitutional obligation of solidarity/protection of man it is possible, on one hand, to accept the request for protection of the individual, and on the other, to increase the level of environmental education of the State's population, guaranteeing the most effective and shared ecosystem protection.

---

inviolable rights of man, both as an individual and in the social formations where his personality takes place and requires the fulfillment of the mandatory duties of political, economic and social solidarity». With regard to considering the environment as a constitutional duty, see F. Fracchia, *La tutela dell'ambiente come dovere di solidarietà,* (Environmental protection as a duty of solidarity), in Diritto dell'Economia, Enrico Mucchi, Modena, 2009.

[34] See F. Gargallo di Castel Lentini, *L'ambiente come diritto fondamentale dell'uomo* (The environment as a fundamental human right), at www.dirittoambiente.com.

In this sense, it is certainly not excluded that local public bodies, also due to a general, increasing economic crisis, partly entrust this task to the citizens themselves through special agreements, implementing the principle of "horizontal" subsidiarity[35] discussed referring to art. 118 of the Constitution.

1.2. The notion of environmental damage: a multiple-offense crime

As mentioned in the introduction, in all international legal documents there is no legal definition of ecological damage, considered as such. The international legal system, in fact, has only defined various causes of damage deriving from pollution, such as, for example, death or personal injury, economic damage, damage to property, costs of preventive measures and recovering damage to natural resources.

To this must be added the lack of a single juridically coercive instrument, such as a treaty, capable of harmonizing the various international sector regulations. Environmental provisions of a general nature, in fact, are only contained in the declarations of principles, that are non-binding legal documents by their nature.

Even the Stockholm declaration on the human environment of 1972, at Principle 22, urged the various Member States to «cooperate to develop further the international law regarding liability and compensation for the victims of pollution and other environmental damage caused by activities within the jurisdiction or control of such States to areas beyond their jurisdiction or under their control». This commitment, however, is still disregarded by the various States.[36]

---

[35] For an understanding of the obstacles that still hinder the full implementation of the principle of horizontal subsidiarity in general, see M. Musella, *La sussidiarietà orizzontale. Economia, politica, esperienze territoriali in Campania* (Horizontal Subsidiarity. Economics, politics, territorial experiences in Campania), Carocci, 2012.

[36] For an in-depth analysis of the aforementioned problems, see the considerations made by S. Poli, *La responsabilità per Danni da inquinamento transfrontaliero nel*

The aforementioned shortcomings have led the European Parliament and Council to approve the Directive 2004/35/EC of 21 April 2004 on the environmental liability with regard to preventing and remedying environmental damages, later implemented within our legal system in the 2006 Environmental Code.

The origins of the European Directive date back to the 1990's, precisely, during the Commission's presentation to the Council, the European Parliament and the Economic and Social Committee of the first general document on civil liability for environmental damage, i.e. the 1993 Green Paper.[37]

This document, of a purely consultative nature, highlighted in its introduction the need for a community intervention that would determine a uniform standard, both to regulate the problems concerning cross-border environmental damages and to harmonize the legislation in force in the Member States.[38]

In this regard, concerns emerged on the harmonization of the law, considered too strict and detailed, which could have limited the competitiveness of European companies.[39] It was assumed that the adoption of a framework directive rather than a regulation would be feasible[40] also to ensure respect for the principle of subsidiarity.[41]

Secondly, the intention of assessing the usefulness of civil liability as a tool to allocate the costs of remedying environmental damage as well as being a disincentive to pollution was highlighted. Furthermore, the possibility of remedying the aforementioned damages was considered through collective compensation systems[42], if the use of this instrument is not possible.

---

diritto comunitario e internazionale (Responsibility for damage caused by cross-border pollution in Community and International law), Milan, 2006.

[37] See Communication from the Council, Parliament and the Economic and Social Committee: Green Paper on civil liability for environmental damage, COM 47 of May 14, 1993, in GUCE n. C / 149 of 29 May 1993.

[38] See the Green Paper, premises, par. 2.3.

[39] See introduction, par. 3.2.4.

[40] See par. 3.6.2.

[41] See par. 3.2.

[42] See par. 3.4.1.

The Paper stressed the need to establish some basic principles concerning the definitions of: environment and environmental damage, restoration, compensation, activities subject to a strict liability system, legitimacy to act, burden of proof and causal link, possibility of defense for the alleged perpetrator, possible role of insurance companies and banks, and lastly, collective compensation systems.[43]

In-depth studies were thus carried out on the various liability systems in force for damage to natural resources, which resulted in the publication of the White Paper on liability for environmental damage in 2000.[44]

The document, which is also non-binding, defined the following important points: strict liability for damage caused by dangerous activities; fault liability for damage caused by non-dangerous activities;[45] application of the aforementioned liabilities to both "traditional damages" (injuries to people and damage to property) and to damage to environmental media similarly to the 1993 Lugano Convention;[46] application of the polluter pays principle according to the effective restoration of contaminated places;[47] obligation for the States to remedy the environmental damage in the event of failure to identify the perpetrator;[48] the right of the individuals or of established groups to replace the authority responsible for environmental damage in case of its inaction;[49] strengthening access to justice,[50] financial guarantee,[51] and lastly, compliance with the principles of subsidiarity and proportionality.[52]

After further research on the subject, in 2002, the Commission presented a proposal for a Directive of the European Parliament and

---

[43] See Green Paper, par. 3.6.1.

[44] Presented by the European Commission, in COM (2000) 66 final, Brussels, February 9, 2000.

[45] See White Paper, conclusions, par. 4.3.

[46] See par. 5.1.

[47] See par. 3.2.

[48] See par. 3.3, par. II.

[49] See conclusions, par. 4.7.2.

[50] See par. 4.7

[51] See par. 4.9.

[52] See par. 6.

Council on environmental liability with regard to the prevention and remedying of environmental damage.[53]

This document, however, deviated from the guidelines of the White Paper since it allowed the application of the civil liability system only for damage to natural media, referring the law on damages against things and people deriving from environmental contamination to the national legislation. Furthermore, the document did not foresee neither the obligation to remedy by the States in the event of non-identification of the operator, nor the obligation to replace them in case of inaction of the authority responsible for the environmental damage.

The document presented, which was inspired by the US environmental liability system based on the *Comprehensive Environmental Response, Compensation and Liability Act of 1980,*[54] provided rules for concrete damage remedy, being decidedly ahead of its time when it was approved.

Compensation for environmental damage, in fact, was conceived only in a specific form also through the restoration of the services of the compromised natural resources, through the methods of resource-resource and service-service equivalence. The monetary assessment, instead, was limited to determining the extent of the remedying measures using the cost-value and value-value methods.

---

[53] In COM (2002) 17 final, Brussels, January 23, 2003. For an analysis of the proposed directive, please refer to C. Clarke, *La proposta della direttiva CE sulla reponsabilità: a metà strada attraverso la procedura di codecisione,* (The Proposal of the EC Liability Directive: halfway through the codecision procedure), in RECIEL, 2003; B. Pozzo, *La proposta di nuova direttiva sulla prevenzione e il risarcimento del danno all'ambiente* (The proposal for a new directive on the prevention and compensation of damage to the environment,) *Danno e Responsabilità* (Damage and Liability), 2002.

[54] See C. Stern Switzer, L.A. Bulan, *CERCLA: Comprehensive Environmental Response, Compensation and Liability Act (Superfund), Section of Environment, Energy, and Resources Book Publications Committee,* 2002; J.R. Mac Ayeal, *The Comprehensive Environmental Response, Compensation, and Liability Act: The correct Paradigm of Strict Liability and the Problem of Individual Causation,* UCLA J. Env. L. & Pol., 2000; P. Grad., *A legislative History of the Comprehensive Environmental Response, Compensation and Liability ("Superfund") Act of 1980,* 8 Colum. J. Env. L., 1, A 1982.

However, differently from the US system, the directive's new setup did not foresee a retroactivity in the individual environmental liability system as this would have had a more onerous impact.

Furthermore, the text urged the Member States to provide a financial guarantee and take preventive and remedial measures if the operator was not identifiable, if he did not have the financial resources or was not held responsible.

Lastly, the States themselves were required to define the public authority responsible for carrying out the tasks provided for by the directive, including the identification of the operator responsible for the ecological damage and the determination of the aforementioned necessary measures.

Thus, on 21 April 2004, the European Council and Parliament reached the approval of Directive 2004/35/EC,[55] through a co-decision procedure pursuant to art. 251 of the then EC Treaty.[56]

---

[55] Published in GUCE series L. 143/56 on 30 April 2004. The directive was later amended by Directive 2006/21/EC on the management of waste from mining industries and amending Directive 2004/35/EC, as well as by Directive 2009/31/EC, on the geological storage of carbon dioxide, modifying the Directives 85/337/EEC, 2000/60/EC, 2001/80/EC, 2004/35/EC, 2006/12/EC, 2008/1/EC and the EC Regulation n. 1013/2006. For a comment on the directive, see B. Pozzo, *La nuova Direttiva 2004/35 del Parlamento Europeo e del Consiglio sulla responsabilità in materia di prevenzione e riparazione del danno* (The new Directive 2004/35 of the European Parliament and of the Council on liability concerning damage prevention and remedy), RGA, 1, 2006; V. Fogleman, *La direttiva sulla responsabilità ambientale* (The Environmental liability Directive), Env. L., 2004; F. Giampietro, *La direttiva n. 2004/35/CE sulla responsabilità per danno all'ambiente messa a confronto con l'esperienza italiana* (The Directive n. 2004/35/EC on liability for damage to the environment compared to the Italian experience), Ambiente 10, 2004; P. Gianpietro, *Prevenzione e riparazione del danno ambientale: la nuova direttiva n. 2004/35/CE,* (Prevention and remedy of environmental damage: the new directive no. 2004/35/EC), Ambiente, 10, 2004; R. Miccichè, *Nuova direttiva europea in materia di responsabilità ambientale* (New European Directive on Environmental Liability), RGA, 2003.

[56] The procedure involving the necessary legislative cooperation between the European Council and Parliament was introduced for the first time by the Treaty of Maastricht in 1992 and later expanded by the Treaty of Amsterdam in 1999. With the entry into force of the Lisbon Treaty in 2009, the co-decision procedure became the main legislative procedure in the EU system.

Moreover, as previously suggested by the Green Paper and then by the White Paper, the adoption of a directive was a more cautious choice as compared to the other option of approving a regulation.

The endorsement of this regulatory instrument, in fact, would have infringed the aforementioned principle of subsidiarity between the Union and the Member States as regards the right of the latter to legislate in competing matters, such as the environmental one, as well as the principle of proportionality as per art. 5.4 of the TFEU.[57]

The regulation is, by definition, «of a general scope. It is binding in its entirety and directly applicable in each Member State».[58]

While the directive is, on one hand, a source of EU law which also has a binding efficacy, on the other, imposes only the obligation of achieving a certain result, leaving the Member State with the right to choose the form and means to implement it.[59]

Moreover, among the preliminary considerations of the directive, was the fact that several Member countries had already endorsed various sector regulations, even if incomplete, or had joined international treaties regulating civil liability in relation to specific sectors.[60]

Considering the above, the directive in question introduced for the first time into the European legal system a detailed definition of environmental damage:

a) *damage to protected species and natural habitats, which is any damage that has significant adverse effects on reaching or maintaining the favorable conservation status of such habitats or species. The significance of such effects is to be assessed with reference to the baseline conditions, taking account of the criteria set out in Annex I;*

b) *water damage, which is any damage that significantly adversely affects the*

---

[57] See Directive 2004/35/EC, recital n. 3, last paragraph. With regard to the principle in question, pursuant to art. 5. 4 of the TFEU «by virtue of the principle of proportionality, the content and form of the Union's action are limited to what is necessary to achieve the objectives of the Treaties».

[58] Treaty on the functioning of the European Union, art. 288. 2.

[59] See art. 288. 3.

[60] See Directive 2004/35/EC, recital n. 12.

ecological, chemical and/or quantitative status and/or the ecological potential, as defined in Directive 2000/60/EC, of the waters concerned with the exception of adverse effects where Article 4 (7) of that Directive applies;

c) *land damage, which is any land contamination that creates a significant risk of human health being adversely affected as a result of the direct or indirect introduction in, on or under land, of substances, preparations, organisms or micro-organisms.*[61]

The natural resources exclusively identified in the aforementioned list,[62] among other things, were meticulously defined with reference to the applicative scope of the directive.

In fact, with regard to the species, reference was made to those mentioned in art. 4, par. 2, of Annex I to Directive 79/409/EEC, and in Annexes II and IV to Directive 92/43/EEC.

Protected natural habitats, instead, are those referred to in art. 4 and Annex I of Directive 79/409/EEC, as well as in Annexes I, II and IV to Directive 92/43/EEC.[63] Lastly, with respect to waters, reference was made to Directive 2000/60/EC,[64] while for the land there were no further specifications with respect to a generic introduction into the soil, on the soil or in the subsoil as provided for by the content of art. 2.1.

Damage from noise and air pollution was however implicitly excluded, excepting cases where it could cause damage to the natural resources listed in art. 2.1,[65] or to the landscape.

Other explicit exclusions were also envisaged, as regards damage to protected species and natural habitats not covered by EU law, according to the national regulations concerning the conservation of nature with an equivalent effect.

Moreover, compared to the provisions of the White Paper, the

---

[61] See Directive 2004/35/EC, art. 2.1.
[62] See art. 2.12.
[63] See art. 2.3, lett. a) and b).
[64] See art. 2.5.
[65] See recital n. 4.

Directive does not apply to individual material or immaterial damage deriving from pollution, except for any right concerning the aforementioned types of damage[66] provided for by national laws.[67]

Actually, with regard to damage to the soil, the provision referred to in letter c) of art. 2.1 expressed a clear anthropic profile: it did not affect the damage to the natural resource in itself, but the negative consequences for human health.

Lastly, after the notion of environmental damage, art. 2.2 also defined the concept of "damage" as «a measurable negative change in a natural resource or a measurable deterioration of the service of a natural resource, which may occur directly or indirectly».

"Service" meaning the function that a natural resource exerts for the benefit of another resource or of the community.[68]

The aforementioned provision that specified the meaning of damage therefore appeared redundant with respect to what had already been stated in the three distinct hypotheses of environmental contamination. Nevertheless, it had the merit of extending its scope also to the services of natural resources, highlighting the aforementioned concept of interrelationship between them and the human being, which is also fundamental for the quantification of the environmental damage, to be discussed later.

In the Italian legal system, the environmental code, which implemented the European directive, has acknowledged the provisions of art. 2.1-2 of the directive, overturning them.

Art. 300 of the Code, in fact, defines first of all an all-encompassing notion of environmental damage through the content of the directive's generic definition of "damage", with the variation of the expression "utility" of a natural resource, without offering an explanation of the content.[69]

---

[66] See Directive 2004/35/EC, recital n. 14.

[67] See art. 3.3.

[68] See art. 2.13.

[69] Art. 300 paragraph I of the Environmental Code clearly states that «environmental

Indeed, among the definitions referred to in art. 302 of the Code,[70] there still is the one relative to a "service",[71] as mentioned in the concept of damage referred to in art. 2.2 of the European directive.

The choice of the national legislator to introduce a generic definition in the first place could be justified by the need to establish a responsibility for the damage to the environment considered in its unity, based on the literature referred to in the previous paragraph.

However, secondly, this general notion of damage to the environment was explained by listing the cases of contamination referred to in the European Directive, such as damage to protected habitats and natural species, to water and to the land.

In this regard, there was an explicit reference to its provisions, where, in paragraph II of Article 300, clearly states that

according to Directive 2004/35/EC, environmental damage is the deterioration, in comparison to the original conditions, caused: a) to the species and natural habitats protected by national and community legislation [. . .]; (b) inland waters, through actions that significantly impact on: (1) the ecological, chemical or quantitative status or ecological potential of the waters concerned, as defined in Directive 2000/60/EC, with the exception of the negative effects to which Article 4, par. (7) of that directive applies; 2) the environmental status of the marine waters concerned, as defined in Directive 2008/56/EC, insofar as particular aspects of the ecological status of the marine environment are not already covered in Directive 2000/60/EC; c) coastal waters and those included in the territorial sea through the aforementioned actions, even if carried out in international waters; (d) to the land, through any contamination creating a significant risk of harmful effects, including indirect effects, on human health following the introduction into the ground, on the soil or in the subsoil of

---

damage is any significant and measurable, direct or indirect deterioration of a natural resource or of the utility assured by the latter».

[70] Art. 302 of the code resumes, albeit with some variations, the definitions as per art. 2 of Directive 2004/35/EC.

[71] Pursuant to art. 302, paragraph XI, «for "services" and "services of natural resources" means the functions performed by a natural resource in favor of other natural resources and/or the public».

substances, preparations, organisms or micro-organisms harmful to the environment.

It should be noted that with art. 25 of Law no. 97[72] of August 6, 2013, the extensive definition of "environmental offense" as contained in the second paragraph of article 311 of the code was deleted: «Anyone who by carrying out an illicit act, or by omitting appropriate activities or behaviors, with violation of the law, of regulations, or of an administrative provision, with negligence, incompetence, imprudence or violation of technical standards, causes damage to the environment, altering it, deteriorating or destroying it in whole or in part, is obliged to restore the previous situation and, failing that, to compensate the State for an equivalent asset».[73]

In Part Six of the Environmental Code itself, therefore, there were two opposite forecasts: one, still in force, was erroneously inspired by the European Directive, defining the cases of environmental contamination with a deductive method; the other, instead, provided a general case of damage to the environment through any unlawful act or negligent omission capable of generating a "negative alteration" to it.

Like in the directive, excluded from the scope of the notion of environmental damage, as per art. 300 of the code, were the aspects concerning the landscape and the cultural profiles, except for indirect protection if they constituted protected natural habitats.

---

[72] Laying down provisions for the fulfillment of obligations deriving from Italy's membership into the European Union - European Law 2013, published in the Official Gazette no. 194 of 20/08/2013.

[73] The provision was based on art. 18 of the Law 349/1986, which defined for the first time an environmental offense in its strict sense: «Any fraudulent or negligent fact that violates legal provisions or measures, that compromises the environment, causing damage to it by altering it, deteriorating it or destroying it in whole or in part, obliges the perpetrator to pay a compensation to the State». The latter rule, in turn, was inspired by art. 2043 of the Civil Code, which instead defines generic "non-contractual" civil offenses, consisting in committing any fraudulent or negligent fact that causes unjust damage, according to which the person responsible for the damage is obliged to pay compensation.

Not even the atmospheric pollution in itself was included, due, probably, to the difficulty in assessing the damage in terms of duration and causal link. The effects of atmospheric pollution on the individual environmental components were therefore assessed, except however in the case of the individual compensation claims. Based on the aforementioned judgment of the Supreme Court no. 440/1989, Article 313, par. VII[74] of the code, in fact, recognized the right to act individually in court against the person responsible for the damage, to persons harmed by a fact generating an environmental damage.

This right was based on art. 2043 of the Civil Code,[75] on condition that those who intended to act provided evidence of having suffered -due to the damaging event- the violation of one of their fundamental rights such as the right to health to which art. 32 of the Constitution refers.

In this regard, an individual action could be implemented by the owner of a fund also as a precautionary measure,[76] particularly through an appeal pursuant to art. 700 of the Civil Code,[77] to request an

---

[74] Article. 3.3 of Directive 2004/35/EC clearly assigns to Member States the possibility of envisaging individual compensation claims deriving from environmental damage or the threat of it: «Without prejudice to the relevant national legislation, this Directive does not give individuals the right to compensation following environmental damage or an imminent threat of such damage».

[75] Pursuant to art. 2043 of the Civil Code, «Any wrongdoing or negligent fact, that causes unjust harm to others, obliges the person who has committed the offense to compensate the damage». It is the so called "*illecito aquiliano*" (*Aquiliano*: from the Lex Aquilia = tort concerning injurious damages). Unlike criminal law, in which all criminally relevant offenses are predefined, in the provision of the article in question any fact can be considered an offense, provided that it generates unjust damage, that is a lesion of a constitutionally guaranteed interest caused in the absence of valid justification.

[76] The precautionary proceedings referred to in Articles 669 et seq. of the Code of Civil Procedure are aimed at ensuring that the right asserted in court, whose existence is considered probable based on a superficial assessment (so called *fumus boni iuris*), does not suffer damage pending the settlement of the dispute (so called *periculum in mora*). These can be activated before or during the main proceedings. Precautionary measures are therefore instrumental and provisional because they are normally replaced by a definitive provision of the judge, delivered at the outcome of the proceedings for merit, cognition or execution.

[77] The instrument of art. 700 of the Code of Civil Procedure can be used for exclusion, if the conditions for the application, also in environmental matters, of the

inhibitory protection of the emissions (smoke, heat, exhalations and similar propagations) that exceeded the threshold of normal tolerability as per art. 844 of the Civil Code. The latter rule, in fact, is aimed at protecting both property and health.[78]

An injunction, therefore, is an action by which the judge is asked to repress a conduct or activity detrimental to an interest susceptible to protection by the legal system. This form of legal protection, of course, can be requested - pursuant to art. 700 of the Civil Code - if the emissions generate a danger of imminent and irreparable damage, or, according to the circumstances of the ecological damage, through other typical remedies. For example, if a mere disruption or impediment occur in the exercise of the right of ownership or possession, an action to quiet title or keep possession - as established respectively in Articles. 949 and 1170 of the Civil Code - can be implemented.

Next to the *Aquiliano* offense pursuant to art. 2043 of the Civil Code, the protection afforded, in particular, by articles 2049, 2050 and 2051 of the Civil Code can reasonably be applied in the cases of "presumed" liability, respectively, of the owners and of the customers for the exercise of dangerous activities and for damage caused by something in custody.

In general, the legal system establishes a typical liability for damage caused to third parties presumably attributed to a certain person -even for indirect liability- who has the right to provide evidence of the act of providence in his defense. Such reversal of the burden of proof constitutes an exception to the system of general non-contractual liability

---

other precautionary measures under art. 669 bis et seq. of the Code are missing: «whoever has founded reasons to fear that during the time necessary to assert his right in an ordinary way, this is threatened by imminent and irreparable damage, can ask the judge for urgent measures, which according to the circumstances, are those most suitable to provisionally ensure the effects of the decision on the merits». For a guide on the use of strategies to obtain precautionary protection pursuant to art. 700 of the Code of Civil Procedure, reference is made to G. Cassano, *La tutela cautelare ex art. 700 c.p.c.* (Precautionary protection pursuant to art. 700 of the Code of Civil Procedure), Maggioli, 2016.

[78] See Supreme Court (*Corte di Cassazione*), judgment no. 8420 of 2006; S.U., judgment no. 10186 of 1998.

as per art. 2043 of the Civil Code, on the basis of which it is for the injured person to prove the unlawful act and the injustice of the damage in order to obtain compensation from the perpetrator. However, the exonerating circumstance is absent in the provision of art. 2049 of the Civil Code, which, therefore, seems to define a real strict liability of the owner or of the customer for damages caused to third parties by their attendants or assistants.

The nature of the presumed liability, in particular that referred to in articles 2049 of the Civil Code et seq., is discussed both in literature and in case-law, which tend to opt for a strict liability,[79] based on the mere existence of a causal link between an illicit fact and a damage-consequence, without detecting the malice or guilt of the perpetrator. Therefore, these liabilities, which are special with respect to the general rule pursuant to art. 2043 of the Civil Code, are opposed to the latter, whose application, subject to the absence of the typical cases, is based on the assumption of guilt or malice of the perpetrator.

Damages of a non-contractual nature suffered by individuals as a result of environmental damage, therefore, can be compensated for the equivalent of the assets, in terms of loss and loss of income as provided for by art. 2056 of the Civil Code,[80] or in a specific form, where possible, through the reinstatement of the condition existing before the damage had occurred pursuant to art. 2058 of the Civil Code.

Furthermore, the same individuals can obtain compensation for non-

---

[79] See Supreme Court (*Corte di Cassazione*), judgment no. 10860 of 2012; no. 4279 of 2008; no. 17471 of 2007; no. 13016 of 1992; no. 778 of 1979. On the topic, see G. Alpa, M. Bessone, *La responsabilità civile*, (Civil Liability) Giuffrè, 2001; S. Rodotà, *Il problema della responsabilità civile* (The Problem of Civil Liability), Milan, 1964; P. Trimarchi, *Rischio e responsabilità oggettiva* (Risk and strict liability), Milan, 1961.

[80] Article 2056 of the Civil Code refers to the application of the provisions on contractual liability contained in articles 1223, 1226 and 1227 of the Civil Code. These rules regulate, respectively, damage compensation with equivalent assets for loss suffered and loss of earnings, the equitable assessment of the damage and concurrence to the offense of the creditor in determining the damage.

pecuniary damages pursuant to art. 2059 of the Civil Code.[81] Such damages may be biological in nature, as a handicap to their psycho-physical integrity, or can affect their quality of life.[82] In this regard, it is right to recall the historical ruling by the Supreme Court (*Corte di Cassazione*) in relation to the Seveso case.

On June 10, 1976, an accident occurred at the ICMESA company's plant in Meda, that caused the dispersion of the toxic chemical dioxin TCDD, that spread over many areas adjacent to the industrial plant, with a main concentration on the city of Seveso. The ecological disaster that ensued created concern among the local population and sparked a media attack against the management of the company and the institutions. A few years later, the European Community decided to take action in a timely manner, endorsing Directive 82/501/EEC of 24 June 1982 on the risks of major accidents associated with certain industrial activities.

In that circumstance, the Supreme Court (*Corte di Cassazione*) recognized that in the event of intentional environmental disaster – pursuant to art. 449 of the Criminal Code[83] – a psychological damage could also be compensated, such as mental anguish or personal suffering, complained of by those who lived or worked in the vicinity of the contaminated place. This was and is possible since the offense in question has a multi-factor character: it can involve both damage to environmental media as well as the independent breach of the fundamental interests of a constitutionally guaranteed individual.[84]

---

[81] Article 2059 of the Civil Code, titled Non-pecuniary damage, expressly reserves the regulation of cases in which non-pecuniary damage must be reimbursed, to the law.

[82] See Supreme Court (*Corte di Cassazione*), judgment no. 20927 of 2015; no. 531 of 2014.

[83] With the entry into force of Law no. 68 of 22 May 2015, title VI bis *Dei delitti contro l'ambiente* (offenses against the environment) was introduced in the Criminal Code. The new criminal environmental legislation, however, presents several substantial critical points. On the topic, see M. Catenacci, *L'introduzione dei delitti contro l'ambiente nel codice penale: Una riforma con poche luci e molte ombre* (The introduction of offenses against the environment in the criminal code. A reform with few lights and many shadows), in *Rivista quadrimestrale di diritto dell'ambiente* (Quarterly review of environmental law), no. 2, 2015.

[84] See Supreme Court (*Corte di Cassazione*), judgment no. 641 of 1987.

For the right to compensation to be recognized by a judge, the injured person must prove that he suffered psychological damage of a transitory nature as mentioned above, due to exposure to the polluting substances.

Such damage can be compensated also independently, regardless of the existence of biological damage or other events generating a pecuniary damage.[85]

The decision of the Court, among other things, is consistent with the case law's orientation that also admits compensation for psychological, non-pecuniary damage claimed by family members of the individual who suffered unintentional injuries[86] as well as independent compensation of the damage itself, regardless of its repercussions at the pecuniary level.[87]

Psychological, non-pecuniary damage is recognized, under certain conditions, even to an individual who deceased due to a damaging event, with the compensation going to his/her heirs.[88]

Moreover, an existential damage understood as the disruption of life habits or normal social life was also affirmed, as a non-pecuniary damage not subject to the limitations of art. 2059 of the Civil Code, if this is the consequence of a breach of the interests of a constitutionally protected human being.[89]

The Criminal Supreme Court (*Corte di Cassazione penale*) also ruled on this issue, through the well-known sentence no. 633 of 2012, which definitively endorsed the principle according to which an individual has

---

[85] See Supreme Court (*Corte di Cassazione*), United Sections, judgment no. 2515 of 2002. On compensation of the psychological damage independently from the biological damage and on the dynamic-relational aspects typical of the existential damage, see Supreme Court (*Corte di Cassazione*), judgment no. 11851 of 2015.

[86] See Supreme Court (*Corte di Cassazione*), judgment no. 1516 of 2001.

[87] See Supreme Court (*Corte di Cassazione*), judgment no. 7713 of 2000.

[88] See Supreme Court (*Corte di Cassazione*), judgment no. 12722 of 2015; no. 15760 of 2006; no. 15022 of 2005.

[89] See Supreme Court (*Corte di Cassazione*), judgment no. 9283 of 2014; S.U., judgments no. 26972; no. 26973; no. 26974; no. 2697 of 2008. This orientation had already been expressed by the Supreme Court (*Corte di Cassazione*) in judgments no. 88 of 1979 and no. 233 of 2003. On the topic, see G. Marcatajo, *Il danno ambientale esistenziale* (Environmental existential damage), Edizioni Scientifiche Italiane, 2016.

the legal standing to engage in legal action can be extended to other interested parties, whether individually or in association, including local public bodies, whose rights have been violated by environmental damage.

In particular, private legal entities and local authorities can take legal action to remedy pecuniary damages related to the ecological damage as such.

These entities shall also be granted damage compensation pursuant to art. 1227 of the Civil Code[90] for damage to their image, also for tourism purposes, with the exclusion of non-pecuniary damages since these can only refer to physical or psychological suffering typical of a physical person.[91]

In this regard, it is assumed that damage to the image of a public body can result in a reduced consideration of the legal entity, both by the physical persons working in the legal entity as by the citizens, individually or in association, with whom the public entity normally interacts.[92]

The same right shall also be attributed to environmental associations claiming material or non-material damages regarding their image, in cases where evidence is adequately provided.[93]

In this regard, to determine the causal link between an offense and a damage-consequence, the general rule of "most likely" established in civil law applies, also referring to the individual cases of civil liability

---

[90] See Supreme Court (*Corte di Cassazione*), judgment no. 14766 of 2007; n. 2570 of 2004.

[91] Pursuant to art. 1227 c.c. «if the fault of the creditor has contributed to the damage, compensation is reduced according to the severity of the fault and the extent of the consequences that derived from it [. . .] Compensation is not due to the damages that the creditor could have avoided by using ordinary diligence».

[92] See Supreme Court (*Corte di Cassazione*), judgment no. 24619 of 2014; no. 4542 of 2012; no. 12929 of 2007.

[93] See Supreme Court (*Corte di Cassazione*), judgment no. 20150 of 2016; no. 29077 of 2013; no. 34761 of 2011.

regulations mentioned above, in which the burden of proof changes.[94]

This is the so-called "relative probability" criteria, which states that to ascertain an etiological link in percentage terms, there must be of a fifty percent plus one probability that the damaging event is a direct consequence of the unlawful act.

This assessment, of course, requires a specific evaluation of all circumstances and the evidentiary results of the specific case.

Unlike the criminal procedural law, the judge may therefore consider the causal link to be proven «even on the basis of proof that makes it probable and even if such proof is not capable of guaranteeing absolute certainty beyond any reasonable doubt».[95]

In conclusion, environmental damage has the nature of public damage, a typical offense pursuant to art. 300 of the Environmental Code, with a multi-offensive characteristic.[96] It can be compensated as such, with the State legitimated to take action in an ordinary or in an administrative way, with a ministerial order.[97]

At the same time, an ecological damage can cause reflected effects in the single juridical sphere of individuals, both as physical or juridical persons, who can be compensated independently (so-called "protection from environmental damage") through the ordinary remedies of civil liability, before an ordinary judge.

---

[94] See Supreme Court (*Corte di Cassazione*), judgment no. 21619 of 2007; S.U., no. 30328 of 2002.

[95] Supreme Court (*Corte di Cassazione*), judgment no. 23933 of 2013.

[96] On this point, G. Alpa, P. Garofoli, *Manuale di diritto civile* (Manual on civil law), Nel Diritto, 2015.

[97] See chapter II, par. 2-3.

Chapter II

COMPENSATION FOR DAMAGE TO NATURAL RESOURCES

2.1. The dual system of liability for the environmental damage

Directive 2004/35/EC for the first time defined a common legislation on environmental liability for EU Member States, both in terms of prevention and for the remedy of environmental damage,[98] based on sustainable development and the international polluter pays principle.[99]

In particular, the supranational system enacted the polluter pays principle to attribute to those responsible for producing the damage to the environment or threatening it, «the costs of prevention and of actions against pollution as defined by the Public Authority in order to keep the environment in an acceptable state».[100]

More specifically, the Recitals contained in the European Directive state the following

an operator who causes environmental damage or creates an imminent threat of such damage should, in principle, bear the cost of the necessary preventive or remedial measures. In cases where a competent authority acts by itself, or through a third party in the place of an operator, this authority should ensure that the costs incurred are reimbursed by the operator. The operators should ultimately also bear the costs of assessing the environmental damage and, potentially, the cost of an evaluation of the imminent threat of such damage.[101]

---

[98] See Directive 2004/35/EC, recital, no. 3.

[99] See recital no. 2.

[100] As defined for the first time by the Organization for Economic Cooperation and Development(OECD), in its Recommendation no. 128 of May 26th, 1972.

[101] Directive 2004/35/EC, recital, no. 3.

These costs, *inter alia*, are identified in detail in Article 2.16 of the Directive: «the costs justified by the need to ensure the proper and effective implementation of this Directive, including the costs of assessing environmental damage, an imminent threat of such damage and alternative measures, as well as administrative, legal and enforcement costs, the costs of data collection and other general costs, in addition to monitoring and supervision costs».

Therefore, applying of the polluter pays principle should not result in the right to negotiate pollution to environmental media through the payment of a fee. On the contrary, it directly imposes the person responsible to bear the costs for preventing and concretely remedying the damage to natural resources, who in the future will be encouraged to carry out practices aimed at minimizing the risks of environmental damage.[102]

The polluter pays principle, furthermore, does not exclude the involvement of the States. In fact, remedying environmental damage can often be substantially difficult, due to the failure in assessing the responsibility of the Nations as well as that of the material authors of the aforementioned damages.

These cases should be considered when the authors are not identifiable or not obliged to implement remedial measures. In this regard, the European Directive allows, but does not require, Member States to approve regulatory provisions binding other parties (for example the States) or the operator to the obligations contained in the Directive.[103]

Nonetheless, outside the euro area, a form of "joint and several" environmental liability of the States was certainly not approved through binding regulatory instruments such as treaties.

The Convention on International Liability for Damage caused by Space Objects[104] is the only international agreement aimed at attributing

---

[102] See Directive 200435/EC, Recital no. 2.
[103] See art. 16.1.
[104] Signed in London, Moscow and Washington on March 29th, 1972.

an environmental liability only to the States, which is also a strict and absolute liability, regardless of negligence or guilt and without exclusions.

In line with other international agreements, the first article of the Convention under letter a) does not define environmental damage per se, but includes in the concept of damage «the loss of life, personal injury or other impairment of health; or loss of or damage to the property of States, or of persons, natural or juridical or property of international intergovernmental organizations».

However, the provision included in the following article clearly indicates that «a launching State shall be absolutely liable to pay compensation for damage caused by its space object on the surface of the earth or to aircraft flight». Said provision directly attributes to the State owning the space object the absolute liability for damages caused both to flying aircrafts as the "earth's surface" in general and, therefore, even if not openly said, also to environmental media.

Furthermore, the document also complies with international practice regarding the measure of damage. Article 12 therein establishes that

The compensation which the launching State shall be liable to pay for damage under this Convention shall be determined in accordance with international law and the principles of justice and equity, in order to provide such reparation in respect of the damage as will restore the person, natural or juridical, State or international organization on whose behalf the claim is presented to the condition which would have existed if the damage had not occurred.

However, in Directive 2004/35/EC, the polluter pays principle is the main criteria for attributing individual liability, which is to say directly to the perpetrator causing the ecological damage or the threat of it.

The liability system for environmental damage provided for therein is dual: for hazardous professional activities[105] which pose a risk to human

---

[105] Defined by art. 2.7 of Directive 2004/35/EC as «any activity carried out in the course of an economic activity, a business undertaking, irrespective of whether its private or public, profit or non-profit character».

health and to the environment, listed in Annex III to the Directive,[106] a system of strict liability was established, based on the mere existence of a causal link between emission[107] and the damage-consequence; while for occupational activities that have the same risk but that are not included in the aforesaid attachment, a liability system is also required that also includes willful misconduct or negligence.[108]

In both cases, the European legislator has provided exemptions for the civil liability of the operator.[109] The latter, therefore, has the right

toprove that the environmental damage or the imminent threat of such damage: a) was caused by a third party and occurred despite the fact that appropriate safety measures were in place; or b) resulted from compliance with a compulsory order or instruction emanating from a public authority other than an order or instruction consequent upon an emission or incident caused by the operator's own activities.[110]

Furthermore, Member Countries can approve regulations allowing the operator to take advantage of the exemption from liability

if the operator proves that a willful or negligent conduct cannot be attributed to him and that the environmental damage has been caused by:

a) an emission or event expressly authorized by, and fully in accordance

---

[106] These activities concern, for example, waste management, the manufacture or treatment or burial or release into the environment or the transport to the site of dangerous substances or preparations, biocides and plant protection products identified in detail in Annex III.

[107] Conceived pursuant to art. 2.8 of the Directive as «the release into the environment, resulting from human activity, of substances, preparations, organisms or micro-organisms».

[108] See recital no. 8–9 and art. 3.

[109] Pursuant to art. 2.6 of the Directive, operator means «any natural or legal, private or public person who operates or controls the occupational activity or, where this is provided for in national legislation, to whom decisive economic power over the technical functioning of such an activity has been delegated, including the holder of a permit or authorization for such an activity or the person registering or notifying such an activity».

[110] Art. 8.3.

with the conditions of an authorization conferred by or given under applicable national laws and regulations which implement those legislative measures adopted by the Community specified in Annex III, as applied at the date of the emission or event;

a) an emission or activity or any manner of using a product in the course of an activity that the operator demonstrates was not considered likely to cause environmental damage according to the state of scientific and technical knowledge at the time when the emission was released, or the activity took place.[111]

Legislation from Member States concerning cost allocation in cases of multiple party causation is also permitted, such as the apportionment of environmental liability between the producer and the user of a product.[112]

Explicitly excluded from the application of the Directive are the ecological damages caused by activities whose main purpose is national defense or international security,[113] as also damages caused by armed conflicts and extraordinary and uncontrollable natural disasters.[114]

Moreover, the provisions of the Directive only apply to damage caused by pollution of a diffuse character, where it is possible to find a causal link between the damage and the activities of an individual operator.[115]

The imminent "threat" of environmental damage is conceived as «a sufficient likelihood that environmental damage will occur in the near future»[116] only if the natural resources in question are among those included in European legislation.

A provision was however included allowing Member Countries to decide whether to apply the provisions of the Directive even to species and natural habitats not identified by the Directive itself in its concept of

---

[111] Directive 2004/35/EC, art. 8.4.

[112] See art. 9.

[113] See recital no. 10.

[114] See art. 4.1, letter a) and b).

[115] See art. 4.5.

[116] See art. 2.9.

environmental damage.[117] The omission of water and soil from this provision, therefore, once again highlights the confused nature of the aforementioned concept.

The document also grants Member States who are contracting parties to the treaties regulating civil liability in specific sectors, to continue to be such, in order to safeguard the uniform application of these treaties.[118]

Therefore, in the event of damages occurring within the scope of the aforementioned agreements, in particular those referred to in Annex IV of the Directive,[119] the EU Member States that have adhered to or intend to adhere to these agreements will apply the liability system established therein regarding traditional damages: damage to property, injury to life and health, economic loss, and lastly the costs of cleaning, restoring, monitoring and assessing the environmental damage. On the contrary, Member Countries will comply with the provisions of the Directive with regard to legislation on strictly environmental damages exclusively identified therein.[120]

Lastly, the provisions of the Directive are non-retroactive and shall not apply to environmental damages if more than thirty years have elapsed since the activity or incident causing it took place.[121]

The Environmental Code only recently acknowledged the criteria for determining the system and attributing the environmental liability provided for by the Directive.

With the aforementioned European Law no. 97 of 2013, in fact, art. 298 *bis* was introduced and the second paragraph of art. 311 of the Code amended, whose provisions now provide for a dual system of strict and negligent liability, in an active or omissible form.

The aforementioned regulatory measure constitutes the last action by the Italian legislator towards the infringement procedure against Italy,[122]

---

[117] See Directive 2004/35/EC, art. 2.3, letter c).

[118] See recital no. 12.

[119] See art. 2.4.

[120] See recital no. 11.

[121] See art. 17.

[122] In particular, no. 2007/4679. Italy took action against this infringement procedure,

through which the European Commission found certain provisions of Part Six of the Code to be incompatibility with the European legislation introduced with Directive 2004/35/EC.

Specifically, the Commission considered the rules for compensation for environmental damage, discussed later on, to be irreconcilable as also the limitation of obligation of compensation only for damages caused by fraudulent or negligent conduct, as provided for in the aforementioned provision in the previous paragraph II of art. 311 of the Code.

As opposed to the Directive, however, here the distinction between strict and negligent environmental liability is dubious.

In art. 298 *bis*, in fact, according to European provisions, the aforesaid distinction is applied based on whether it is environmental damage or an imminent threat of it caused by a hazardous professional activity,[123] as per Annex 5 to Part Six of the code, or by an occupational activity not included in that Annex.

In both cases, liability is attributed to the operator, meaning the person who carries out a professional activity of "environmental relevance";[124] the latter specification, however, is not present in the notion of operator referred to in the European directive.

Pursuant to art. 311, however, which introduces the compensatory action, a generic liability for environmental damage is clearly attributable to "anyone", regardless of his being qualified as an operator or his

---

with the corrections made by art. 5 *bis*, of Legislative Decree no. 135 of 2009. The EU Commission, however, contested the aforementioned modifications through two substantiated opinions, respectively, of 23 November 2009 and 26 January 2012. This led to the approval of European Law no. 97 of 2013, which only partially introduced the changes to the Environmental Code wanted by the Commission.

[123] Understood, pursuant to paragraph V of art. 302 of the Environmental Code, as «any action, by which profit can be pursued, carried out in the course of an economic, industrial, commercial, handcraft, agricultural and services activity, whether public or private».

[124] The operator is clearly defined in paragraph IV of art. 302 of the Code as «any natural or legal, public or private person, who operates or controls the occupational activity having environmental relevance, or to whom decisive economic power over the technical functioning of such an activity has been delegated, including the holder of a permit or authorization for such an activity».

exercising a professional (nonhazardous) activity of environmental relevance.[125]

However, similarly to the European Directive, art. 308, paragraph IV states that the operator is not required to bear the costs of precautionary, preventive and remedial measures if he can show that the environmental damage or the threat of it «was caused by a third party and occurred despite the existence of abstractly suitable security measures».

Moreover, the subsequent paragraph V provides for additional exemptions if the operator gives evidence

that the fraudulent or negligent conduct and the preventive measure for environmental protection have been caused by:
a) an expressly permitted emission or occurrence;
b) an emission or activity or any other use of a product during an activity where the operator demonstrates that this was not considered likely to cause environmental damage according to the scientific and technical knowledge existing at the time of the emission or execution of the activity.

The aforementioned exemptions of liability for environmental damage are also added to the general exclusions provided for in all of Part Six of the Code, as per art. 303.

In particular, in addition to the non-application of the legislation on the right to compensation in cases of armed conflict, natural disasters and similar occurrences, its non-retroactivity was also confirmed, without prejudice only to the criteria for determining the compensation obligation and to a limitation period for compensation for an environmental damage set at thirty years from its occurrence.

Moreover, the aforementioned legislation shall not be applied to widespread pollution, if it is not possible to ascertain the causal link between the activities and pollution, in application of the key principle of the polluter-pays liability principle.[126]

---

[125] See Environmental Code, articles 298 *bis,* paragraph I, and 311, paragraph II.
[126] A similar provision is included in art. 4, paragraph V of the European Directive 2004/35/EC, where it is stated that in the event of widespread pollution, the Directive

In this regard, it is useful to mention the well-known verdict C-378/08 of 2010,[127] with which the European Court of Justice provided important information to interpret the aforementioned principle in order to determine the causal link.

In particular, the criteria used by the EU Court of Justice was based on the premise that not all forms of contamination can be remedied through civil liability.

For this legal instrument to be effective, it is essential to find a causal link between one or more identifiable operators and the environmental damage, which however must be quantifiable.

Proof of a causal link is required by competent authorities to levy remedial measures against the physical or juridical persons causing the damage, regardless of the type of damage caused to natural resources. Likewise, this obligation is a prerequisite to apply the European Directive also in the cases of widespread environmental damage. Therefore, the Directive applies to this form of pollution only when it is possible to demonstrate a causal link between the damages and the activities of the various operators.

The European Directive, however, does not provide any element to establish a similar causal link. Accordingly, in the Court's view, in the context of a shared jurisdiction between the Union and the Member States in the environmental field, when an element necessary for the implementation of a Directive has not been defined, the State is required to determine this definition.

Furthermore, Member States are granted ample discretionary power, in accordance with the provisions of the Treaty, aimed at adopting national laws that specifically govern the polluter pays principle. In this

---

shall apply only when it is possible to determine the causal link between the damage and the activity carried out by the individual operators in compliance with the polluter pays principle established in art. 174 of the European Union Treaty and in art. 191 of the Treaty on the functioning of the European Union.

[127] Verdict of the EU Court of Justice of 9 March 2010 regarding the proceedings CC–378, 379, 380/08 (Sicily Region vs Raffinerie Mediterranee ERG, Polimeri Europa S.p.A and Syndial S.p.A).

regard, the Court considers that «the Directive does not exclude any national legislation allowing the competent authority, when implementing the aforementioned directive, to presume the existence of a causal link, even in the case of widespread pollution, between certain operators and an established pollution, on the basis of the proximity of their plants to the polluted area».

According to the polluter pays principle, however, the remedy obligation is attributed to the operators only to an extent corresponding to their causal contribution in determining the environmental damage or the threat of it.

In order to be able to presume the existence of a causal link, the competent authority must use plausible indications to justify this presumption, such as the proximity of the operator's plant to the pollution site and the correspondence between the pollutants found and the components used by that operator in the exercise of his activity.

The criteria can also be applied to the provisions of Directive 2004/35/EC, provided that the operators are not able to overcome the aforementioned presumption.

Therefore, only in this way can the legislation of a Member State establish that the competent authority may impose measures to prevent and remedy the established environmental damage.

Moreover, when the competent authority decides to impose preventive or remedial measures to operators whose activities are listed in Annex III of the Directive, the authority is not required to prove either the intent or fault of the latter, deeming sufficient the existence of a causal link based on the aforementioned criteria.

According to the EU Court of Justice, therefore, the polluter pays principle is interpreted to mean that environmental liability should be channeled to the operator, based on the existence of a link between the activities exercised by him and the damage to the natural resources.

The assessment of the causal link is always necessary, even in cases of strict liability for damage from hazardous activities, as per Annex III of Directive 2004/35/EC, which is unrelated to the finding of willful misconduct or negligence. This connection can be presumed on the basis of the proximity between the damage and the polluting activity (and between different operators) and of the correspondence between the pollutants found and those used by the operator's activities.

Only based on this specific data, can the uncertain data on the liability among several operators be ascertained, unless there is particularly rigorous evidence showing that they have used all the measures necessary to prevent pollution, to the point of demonstrating the occurrence of a force majeure event.

Additionally, in the event that the damage spreads beyond the national borders but remains limited to the territory of the European Union, the Minister of the Environment is obliged to cooperate, also through a suitable exchange of information, to ensure the successful completion of actions to prevent and repair the damage to natural resources.

When the damage originates in territories of the Italian State, the Minister of the Environment shall inform the Member States that they could be exposed to its effects. If on the other hand, the environmental damage identified within the national boundaries was caused beyond its boundaries, the Minister shall inform the European Commission and other potentially interested States and may, if necessary, recommend the adoption of preventive or remedial measures.[128]

Lastly, please note that in the aforementioned European law of 2013, the letter i) of art. 303 of the Code, was eliminated.[129]

---

[128] See the Environmental Code, art. 318, paragraph IV, implementing art. 15 of Directive 2004/35/EC.

[129] This correction was imposed by the EU Commission in the context of the infringement procedure no. 2007/4679. The Commission, in fact, argued that the suppressed provision was not included in the provisions of Article 4 of Directive 2004/35/EC, and that the Italian authorities had not provided clarifications regarding the scope of art. 303, lett. i), of the Environmental Code; in particular, this referred to the purpose of defining the application scope of the various legislations envisaged by the Environmental Code on the subject of clearing and remedying environmental damage. See, Supplementary motivated opinion of the European Commission of 26 January 2012, *parte in diritto*, lett. C) «The exclusion provided for by art. 303, letter i), of Legislative Decree 152/2006: violation of articles 3 and 4 of the Directive».

This provision excluded applying the norms on environmental damage in cases of contamination where reclamation procedures had already started, or when the sites referred to in art. 239 *et seq.* of the code had been remedied, except for the persistence of an environmental damage even after these procedures.

With this, the national legislator left a flaw open in the system of liability for environmental damage, since, as will be observed when speaking of damage quantification, the two different legislations have opposing elements that create uncertainties on the application of their provisions.

2.2. Prevention and remedial measures

According to the European Environmental Liability Directive, in the case of a damage threat, the operator is obliged to adopt the necessary preventive measures, i.e. the actions necessary[130] to address the threat, in order to prevent or minimize ecological damage.[131]

In any case, the competent authority can request information to the identified operator, ordering him to adopt the aforementioned measures or to undertake them directly, without prejudicing the right of recourse against the liable party within a five-year limitation period.[132]

Similar rules, moreover, apply to the remedial action for environmental damage,[133] understood as «any action or combination of actions, including mitigating or interim measures to restore, rehabilitate or replace damaged natural resources and/or impaired natural services, or to provide an equivalent alternative to these resources or services, as provided for in Annex II».[134]

---

[130] See Directive 2004/35/EC, art. 5.1.
[131] See art. 2.10.
[132] See articles 5.3-4 and 10.
[133] See art. 6.2-3.
[134] Art. 2.11.

However, unlike in the prevention measures, the operator must first implement measures to contain the damage, then notify the competent authority and agree upon, pursuant to art. 7, the remedial actions to be undertaken through the restoration[135] or replacement of the damaged natural resources or their services, as per Annex II, par. 2.

Generally, the physical or juridical persons,[136] who are or could be[137] affected by an environmental damage, can solicit the action of the competent authority[138] by filing complaints accompanied by all the data and information relevant to the case. The latter may accept or reject the request for action, substantiating its choice and informing the aforementioned persons according to the procedures established by national laws.[139]

Against the rejection of a request for action, in addition to the illegitimacy of acts or omissions by the competent authorities, the review of an independent and impartial judicial authority is guaranteed. In this regard, the Directive is without prejudice to the laws of the Member States having as their object access to justice and the start of proceedings once the administrative procedures have been completed.[140]

On the other hand, within the Italian legal system, all the regulations on the prevention and remediation of environmental damage included in the Environmental Code are based upon the obligation of applying the international precautionary principle.[141]

---

[135] Pursuant to art. 2.15 of the Directive 2004/35/EC, «"restoration", including "natural restoration" is intended as: in the case of water, of protected species and natural habitats, restoring the natural resources and/or damaged services to their original conditions and, in case of damage to the soil, the elimination of any significant risk of causing adverse effects on human health».

[136] In particular, non-governmental organizations that promote environmental protection pursuant to art. 12. 1, lett. c), of the Directive.

[137] Art. 12.5 of the Directive submits the decision to extend the provisions in question to the Member States, also in the cases of environmental damage threats.

[138] See recital no. 25-26 and art. 12.1-2.

[139] See art. 12.4.

[140] See art. 13.1-2.

[141] See the Environmental Code, art. 301. On the precautionary principle, see P. Pallaro, *Il principio di precauzione tra mercato interno e commercio internazionale: un'analisi del suo ruolo e*

This principle, in coping with the identification of a risk for the environment or human health, requires the adoption of certain cautionary measures, even if the risk's actual evolution into damage cannot be demonstrated based on current scientific knowledge.[142]

In this regard, Principle 15 of the Rio Declaration states that «in order to protect the environment, the precautionary approach shall be widely applied by the States according to their capabilities. Where there are threats of serious or irreversible damage, lack of full scientific certainty shall not be used as an excuse for postponing cost-effective measures to prevent environmental degradation».

The principle in question was later confirmed by article 174 of the EC Treaty, becoming a general principle of the European law, later conveyed into art. 191 of the TFEU.

In this regard, despite various corrections made by the Italian legislator until 2015, the provision of art. 301, Paragraph I, of the Environmental Code does not appear to have been updated with the entry into force of the Treaty of Lisbon, as it refers to the application of the precautionary principle «pursuant to art. 174 paragraph 2 of the EC Treaty».

Aside from these minor details, the provision in question requires that the operator concerned inform the competent authorities and the Minister of the Environment about the risk. The Minister himself has the authority to undertake preventive measures[143] and to promote «information to the public on the negative effects of a product or process, and taking into account the financial resources provided for under the current legislation,

---

del suo contenuto nel diritto comunitario (The precautionary principle between the domestic market and international trade: an analysis of its role and content in EC law), in Dir. Comm. Internaz., 2002; F. Acerboni, *Contributo allo studio del principio di precauzione: dall'origine nel diritto internazionale a principio generale dell'ordinamento* (Contribution to the study on the precautionary principle: from its origin in international law to being a general principle in the legal system), in Dir. Reg., 2000.

[142] See the indications provided in the Notice dated 2 February 2000 of the EC on the precautionary principle [COM (2000) 1 final of 2 February 2000] at www.reteambiente.it.

[143] See the Environmental Code, art. 301, par. III and IV.

he can finance research programs, arrange for the use of environmental certification systems and carry out any other initiative to reduce the threats of environmental damage».[144]

A clear reference to the complementary principle of prevention therefore emerges from the provisions of art. 301, also of an international origin.[145] Unlike that of precaution, the concept of prevention refers to the prediction of scientifically ascertainable threats and their consequent limitation or elimination.

The principle in question is implicitly expressed in the ban to cross-border pollution, ratified for the first time in international law in the previously mentioned Trail case.

The Stockholm Declaration on the Human Environment of 1972 also ruled accordingly, where under principle 21 it also stated that, «in accordance with the Statute of the United Nations and the principles of international law, the States have the sovereign right to exploit their resources pursuant to their environmental and land development policies, and the duty to ensure that the activities carried out within their jurisdiction or control shall not cause damage to the environment of other States or to regions that are not subject to any national jurisdiction».

The same rule was then reiterated in the Rio Declaration on Environment and Development of 1992,[146] as well as in various binding international instruments on the environment, including the Rio Convention on Biodiversity of 1992[147] and the United Nations Framework Convention on Climate Change of 1994.[148]

---

[144] Environmental Code, Art. 301, par. V.

[145] See, T. Daddi, *La prevenzione integrata dell'inquinamento e la gestione ambientale d'impresa. Applicazione della direttiva IPPC/IED ed effetti sulle imprese,* (Integrated prevention to pollution and the environmental management of a company. Application of the *IPPC/IED* Directive and its effects on companies), FrancoAngeli, 2014; G. Mancini Palamoni, *Il principio di prevenzione,* (The principle of prevention) in AmbienteDiritto.it, ISSN 1974–9562, of Nov. 26, 2014.

[146] Rio Declaration on Environment and Development, principle no. 2.

[147] See the Rio Convention on Biodiversity, art. 3.

[148] See UN Framework Convention on Climate Change, preliminary considerations, paragraph VIII.

Lastly, the principle of prevention is ratified in Article 174 of the EU Treaty.

In the Environmental Code, among the definitions included in art. 302, preventive measures are considered «the actions taken to respond to an event, act or omission that creates an imminent threat of environmental damage, in order to prevent or minimize such damage».[149]

In this respect, art. 304, which introduces Title II on prevention and environmental restoration, establishes that in the case of an imminent threat of environmental damage, the operator must take measures within twenty-four hours to prevent the damage from materializing. Therefore, this provision presumably identifies the operator as being responsible, regardless of the type of professional activity carried out.

The adoption of the aforementioned measures must be preceded by a detailed notice on the circumstances pertaining to the existing danger to the competent authorities: the municipality, the province, the region, or the autonomous province in whose territory the damaging event is expected, and the province's Prefect, who must then inform the Minister of the Environment and Protection of the Territory and Sea within the subsequent twenty-four hours.

If the operator does not carry out operations to prevent damage or does not give notice to the aforementioned authorities, the Minister of the Environment or the institution responsible for control may impose a financial administrative fine,[150] ranging from one thousand to thirty thousand euro for each day of delay.[151]

Furthermore, the third paragraph of this same article states that the Minister has the authority to request information on the danger of

---

[149] Environmental Code, art. 302, paragraph VIII.

[150] This is the typical legislative provision issued against a person who has committed an administrative offense. This provision was already included in Law no. 689, of November 24, 1981.

[151] See the Environmental Code, art. 304, paragraph I and II.

environmental damage to the operator, ordering that he undertake preventive measures following certain procedures, or implement the preventive operations himself.

However, the last paragraph establishes that

if the operator does not comply with the obligations laid down in paragraph 1 or paragraph 3, letter b), or if he cannot be identified, or is not required to sustain the costs pursuant to Part Six of this decree, the Minister of the Environment and Protection of the Territory and Sea has the right to take the necessary measures to prevent the damage, approving expenses, with a right of recourse against those who caused or contributed to cause these costs, if identified within five years from the payment.

The same system, albeit with some variations, is covered again in the subsequent art. 305 for the restoration of damage caused to the environment, which essentially follows the European provisions relative to remedial actions.

The same provision establishes, under paragraph I, that in the event of environmental contamination, the operator must immediately inform the authorities of all circumstances regarding the harmful event, with the same effects as in the previous article. Furthermore, the operator is obliged to implement any measure aimed at containing the damage and preventing any further propagation that would be harmful to the environment, as well as to implement the restoration measures established by the Minister, even conventionally, under the subsequent art. 306, unless such measures are necessary and urgent.

The article in question also gives the authority to the Minister to request information from the operator, order him to adopt the appropriate containment and/or restoration measures and to directly implement the aforementioned measures.[152] If the operator does not fulfill these obligations or has not been identified or is not required to bear the costs of containment-restoration measures, the Minister for the Environment

---

[152] See the Environmental Code, art. 305, paragraph II.

can adopt them directly, approving the list of expenses and with right of recourse against the operator who may possibly be identified.[153]

Moreover, according to the subsequent art. 306, the Minister may determine the priority order of the remedial actions if there are several cases of environmental damage and the Authority itself is not «able to ensure the simultaneous adoption of the necessary restoration measures»[154] especially with regard to risks to human health.[155]

In any case, any resolution taken by the competent authority which imposes that the operator (identified by means of preliminary administrative procedures) adopt precautionary, preventive and recovery measures, must be adequately motivated and must indicate the terms with which the operator can exercise the rights of appeal.[156]

These are the so-called "Remedial sanctions", which

affect the object of the offense, bringing the situation back to how it previously was [. . .] these measures are directed towards those liable for the violations [. . .] moreover, a remedial sanction is the most serious punishment and, therefore, it applies to violations of particular gravity, which cannot be remedied, or which affect especially important assets. This explains the different application scope of these sanctions in urban planning and environmental matters, where there is greater inflexibility.[157]

It should be noted that the provisions examined, that have a European origin, present similarities - particularly referring to the restoration order - with the provisions drafted by the national legislator on the administrative compensatory actions referred to in articles 312 and et. seq. of the code, which will be discussed in the following paragraphs.

---

[153] See the Environmental Code, art. 305, paragraph III.

[154] See art. 306, paragraph III. This provision is justified as per Recital no. 17 of Directive 2004/35/EC.

[155] See art. 306, Paragraph IV.

[156] See art. 307, implementing art. 11.4 of the European Directive.

[157] See F. Caringella, *Compendio di diritto amministrativo* (Summary of Administrative Law), Dike Giuridica, 2016.

The aforementioned similarities are confirmed by the provision in art. 314, paragraph VI, where it is clearly stated that «the ministerial orders referred to in articles 304, paragraph 3, and 313 indicate the means for recourse and their relative terms».

The provision, therefore, included in Title III, Part Six, of the Code, concerning the compensation for environmental damage, reiterates what has just been examined by art. 307, contained in Title II regarding prevention and restoration, thus finding application to the ordinances that impose both prevention measures and compensation for ecological damage to the identified operator.

The (implicit) exclusion of the ordinances pursuant to art. 305 from art. 314, Paragraph VI, suggests a substantial equivalence of the restoration and environmental compensation as well as of the relative ministerial ordinances. Such equivalence is confirmed, among other things, by the provision of art. 298 *bis*, paragraph II which states that «the environmental damage must be remedied in compliance with the principles and criteria established in Title II and in Annex 3 to Part Six», i.e. on the basis of the provisions foreseen for restoration and compensation of environmental damage.

Therefore, the provision of art. 312, paragraph I, according to which the preliminary activity aimed at adopting the ministerial ordinance pursuant to art. 313 must take place according to the rules of Law 241/1990, can also be applied to articles 304 and 305 of the Code. Moreover, article 299, included in Title I, concerning the application scope of Part Six of the Code, expressly provides for the Minister's administrative action, who, for preliminary activity, can avail himself of the collaboration of public and private sector experts, though limited to the administration's financial resources.[158]

All this emphasizes once again the fragmented nature of the systematics used in Part Six of the Environmental Code.[159]

---

[158] See the Environmental Code, art. 299, paragraphs II-IV.
[159] See art. 314, paragraph VI.

Furthermore, pursuant to the new art. 306 bis[160], the Minister can first of all settle[161] the pending issue with the operator liable, limited to the case of contamination of a site of national interest.

In particular, based on the first paragraph of the provision in question, the identified operator who was ordered by the Minister to carry out the reclamation or remedy the damage or against whom he has undertaken relevant legal action, has the right to propose a settlement agreement.

Although the new provision still refers to the repealed articles 18, Law 349/1986, and 17, Leg. Decree 22/1997[162], the settlement proposal shall:

a) identify primary, complementary and compensatory remedial measures;
b) take into account the time needed to achieve the objective of the primary or primary/complementary remedy, where compensatory remedy is conceived;
c) provide for a damage settlement through an economic assessment where the resource-resource and service-service criteria are not applicable to determine complementary and compensatory measures;
d) in any case provide for monitoring and control if the impossibility of primary remedy results in residual pollution posing a health and environmental risk;
e) keep into consideration the already approved and implemented reclamation measures pursuant to Title V of Part Four of this decree;
f) have the possibility of being submitted only by a few persons, with

---

[160] Provision included in art. 31 of the Law no. 221 of December 28, 2015, which lays down the *Environmental provisions to promote green economy measures and to contain the excessive use of natural resources,* Gazzetta Ufficiale no. 13 of January 18, 2016.

[161] According to the ruling of art. 1965 of the Civil Code «the transaction is the contract with which the parties, making mutual concessions, place an end to a dispute already begun or prevent a dispute that may arise between them [. . .] With the reciprocal concessions, it is possible to create, modify or extinguish relationships different from that which has been the object of the claim and the contestation of the parties».

[162] The entire legislative decree was repealed by art. 264 of the Environmental Code.

regard to the entire obligation, even when several persons have contributed to causing the damage, thus having reclamation obligations, without prejudice to the right of recourse towards the other persons;

g) provide indications of suitable financial guarantees.[163]

Letter c) of the aforementioned list clearly refers to compensation for damage to environmental media to be paid with an equivalent asset even though on a residual basis.

This is in contrast not only with the provisions of Directive 2004/35/EC, which, as will be seen in the following paragraph, do not include the aforesaid form of restoration, but also with the polluter pays principle, according to which the mere negotiation for the payment of the fee for pollution to environmental media is excluded.

Such a concept, in fact, would favor the wealthiest perpetrators and would hinder the double deterring and incentivizing function of this principle, as expressly referred to in Recitals 2 and 16 as well as in art. 2.16 of the European Directive.

The purpose of the sums that the operator is obliged to pay, in fact, must always be to bear the costs of measures taken to remedy the damage. These measures must be implemented directly by the operator or, failing that, optionally by the Minister, who, only after carrying out the remedial measures, can demand reimbursement of the sums paid to the person liable for the damage, upon notification of an expense report.[164]

Moreover, there are no rules regarding the discretion through which the Minister can assess the existence of the requirements for a settlement agreement proposal.

---

[163] Environmental Code, art. 306 *bis,* paragraph II.
[164] See Environmental Code, Articles 304 and 305; Directive 2004/35/EC, Articles 8.2 and 10.

After his assessment and with a decree, the Minister shall declare the aforesaid proposal admissible or shall reject it due to the lack of the requirements described in the paragraph above.

If the proposal is admissible, within thirty days the Minister will summon a *Conferenza dei servizi*, (meeting of the authorities involved) in which the Region and the interested local public bodies will participate, receiving the opinion of the Supreme Institute for Environmental Protection and Research (ISPRA) and of the Italian National Institute of Health.

The Conferenza summoning will be given appropriate publicity thus allowing all interested parties to present their arguments and observations.

Conferenza dei Servizi will then approve, reject or modify the settlement agreement proposal within one hundred and eighty days from its summoning.

The Conferenza's final decision will be notified to the proposing operator for acceptance, which must take place within the following sixty days. Such resolution shall supersede to all effects all decisions howsoever named and made by the competent authorities called to participate in the aforementioned Conferenza.

Only after acceptance shall the competent authority draw up a draft settlement agreement which must be submitted to the opinion of the Attorney General's Office.

In the event of a positive outcome, the draft settlement agreement must first be signed by the operator and subsequently be subjected to a preliminary legitimacy check by the Court of Accounts pursuant to art. 3, paragraph I of Law no. 20, of January 14, 1994.

If the settlement agreement has the adequate requirements, it will have legal validity between the contracting parties. Therefore, in the event of non-fulfillment by the operator, even partial, the Minister, after issuing a warning to abide within 30 days and enforcing the guarantee and the amount thereof,[165] can declare the settlement agreement terminated and retain the sums already paid by the operator as a down payment of the amounts due for remedying the environmental damage.[166]

Ruling out the possibility of settling the pending issue pursuant to art. 306 *bis*, if the Minister has directly implemented the necessary environmental measures, art. 308, paragraph I establishes that the operator must bear the costs of such initiatives.

In this case, the competent authority «recovers, also through collateral or enforceable first demand bank guarantees and with the exclusion of the right to prior enforcement», the money used for the actions by the identified operator.[167]

The Regions, local authorities, physical or juridical persons have in any case the power to encourage an action by the Minister, as they can lodge complaints and observations with the Prefectures and territorial governmental Offices, accompanied by suitable substantiating documentation concerning any case of environmental damage or the imminent threat of it.[168]

The same persons are also entitled to act before an administrative judge «for the annulment of the deeds and measures adopted in violation of the provisions of Part Six of this decree and against the tacit non-fulfillment of the Minister of Environment and the Protection of the

---

[165] Pursuant to art. 1454 of the Civil Code «where a party fails to perform an obligation, the other party may give written notice to do so within a reasonable time, stating that if, at the end of that period, the notice has not been complied with, the contract will be considered terminated [. . .] Such period may not be less than two weeks, unless the parties agree otherwise or a shorter period is sufficient by reason of the type of contract or common usage [. . .] If the contract has not been performed within that period, it shall be terminated by operation of law».

[166] See the Environmental Code, art. 306 *bis*, paragraphs III-VIII. For a critical analysis of the aforementioned provisions, see V. Cavanna, A. Quaranta, *La nuova transazione ambientale: il legislatore spariglia le carte?* (The new environmental settlement agreement: is the legislator changing the game?) in Ambiente & Sviluppo, no. 4/2016.

[167] See art. 308, paragraph II. This provision reflects the one pursuant to art. 8. 2 of the Directive.

[168] See art. 309, paragraph I.

Territory and the Sea and for the compensation of the damage suffered due to the delay in the activation, by the Minister, of precautionary, prevention or containment measures for the environmental damage».

The aforementioned complaint may also be preceded by an objection filed with the Ministry itself no later than thirty days from the notification, notice or acknowledgement of the deed.[169]

Lastly, in any case, all this is without prejudice to filing an extraordinary complaint to the President of the Republic within one hundred and twenty days from the notification or knowledge of the deed or administrative measure that is deemed illegitimate and harmful.[170]

2.3. Compensatory actions

Directive 2004/35/EC requires Member States to identify the competent authority to perform the tasks therein, in particular to identify the person liable for the environmental damage or the threat of it, to assess the damage and to determine the related remedial measures according to the rules set out in Annex II of this directive.[171]

The States may then also regulate the cases in which the designated authority can delegate or entrust third parties with taking the necessary measures to prevent or remedy environmental damage.[172]

Pursuant to art. 10, the competent authority can initiate against the person liable or the third party (if the conditions exist), proceedings aimed at recovering the costs of the aforesaid measures that were not undertaken by the first two parties, within five years from the end of their implementation or from the moment these costs were identified. Such recovery, however, can also occur through the enforcement of

---

[169] See the Environmental Code, art. 310, paragraph I and II.
[170] See art. 310, paragraph IV.
[171] See Directive 2004/35/EC, recital no. 15 and art. II.I.
[172] See art. 11.2-3.

collaterals or bank guarantees.[173]

In general, as discussed above, those who are or could be harmed by environmental damage may request an action by the competent authority through a formal complaint. Said authority has the right to accept or reject the request, justifying its decision and informing the aforementioned persons in accordance with the laws of the Member States.[174]

Against the rejection, and the illegitimacy of acts and omissions by the competent authority, a review by an independent and impartial judicial authority must always be guaranteed. Member States are also able to, among other things, endorse provisions concerning access to justice and the start of proceedings upon completion of the appeals through administrative procedure.[175]

In the Italian legal system, the first step towards considering an environmental offense within a judicial context is to be attributed to the Court of Auditors, which stated that «damage to the environment affects the interests of the community and may be compensated in an equitable manner, according to the principles of judgment before the Court of Auditors».[176]

Later, with the entry into force of Law 349/1986, environmental damage was excluded from the criteria that included the loss of revenue subject to the jurisdiction of the Court and part of the general legislation on unlawful acts referred to in art. 2043 of the Civil Code, under the jurisdiction of an ordinary judge.

The Court of Auditors still had jurisdiction – as per art. 22, Presidential Decree no. 3 of 1957 – to judge the right of recourse in the cases in which the administration had reimbursed a third party for the damages suffered, due to the action of one of its employees closely related to an environmental damage.

---

[173] See Directive 2004/35/EC, art. 8.2.

[174] See art. 12.4.

[175] See art. 13.1-2.

[176] Court of Auditors, judgment no. 86 of 1980.

Legitimacy to take action, even before a criminal court, for the compensation of damage caused to the environment, was then granted in a concurrent or substitutive way to the State and Local Public Bodies in whose territory the damaged assets were found, consistently with the principle of subsidiarity as per art. 118 of the Italian Constitution.

Citizens and national environmental protection associations, on the other hand, were granted the right to request the previously mentioned action by formally reporting potentially damaging facts to environmental media or any damage to it that they had become aware of.[177]

On this point, the Constitutional Court, considering unfounded the question of constitutional illegitimacy submitted by the Court of Auditors in relation to art. 18, second paragraph, of the same law and to articles 5, 25, paragraph I and 103, paragraph II of the Constitution, made the following decision:

The liability occurring is correctly included within the framework and in the scheme of the Aquilian Liability (Article 2043 of the Civil Code) (*T.N.: Aquiliano:* from the Lex Aquilia = tort concerning injurious damages). The damage is certainly material, though not linked to an arithmetical-accounting concept, and materializes in the economic relevance that the destruction or deterioration or alteration or, in general, prejudice to the asset in itself and for itself reflects on the community, that is burdened with economic costs. The consideration that the right to damage compensation arises only after financial accounting loss in the institution's balance sheet, namely from damage to the institution's assets, with no effect on State owned assets, was no longer valid. The legitimacy to act attributed to the State and to smaller bodies, is not founded on the fact that they have incurred expenses to remedy the damage or on the fact that they have suffered an economic loss, but in their capacity to protect the public and communities in their own territory and the interests of the ecological, biological and sociological balance of their territory.[178]

---

[177] See Law no. 349 of 1986, art. 18, paragraphs II-IV.
[178] Constitutional Court, judgment no. 641 of 1987.

With the entry into force of the Environmental Code in 2006, following the constitutional reform no. 3 of 2001, where the State was assigned exclusive environmental protection, and having established its importance as a widespread interest, only the Minister of the Environment had legal standing with regard to the compensation for environmental damage.[179]

The code, however, has left in force the fifth paragraph of art. 18, according to which the national environmental protection associations can take part in the compensation proceedings for environmental damage and appeal before the administrative judge to obtain the annulment of illegitimate administrative acts.[180]

The aforementioned provisions, moreover, have recently received the final approval of the Constitutional Court, that referred to the norms of Directive 2004/35/EC and its previous judgment no. 235 of 2009, according to which

the decision to assign the administrative functions to the state administration is reasonably justified by the need to ensure that the prevention and remedy task for an environmental damage shall meet uniformity and unity criteria, given that the environmental protection level cannot vary in the various different areas and also considering the common and cross-border nature of the ecological problems, according to which the effects of environmental damage cannot easily be limited within a precise and restricted territorial area.[181]

In this regard, art. 299 of the Code, included in Title I, which defines Part Six's scope of application in issues concerning the right to compensation for ecological damage, in the first paragraph explicitly attributes to the Minister the functions concerning the protection, prevention and remedy of environmental damage, also in collaboration with other public bodies: the Regions, local authorities and any public law body deemed appropriate.

---

[179] See the Environmental Code, art. 311, paragraph I.
[180] See art. 318, paragraph II, letter a).
[181] Constitutional Court, judgment no. 126 of 2016.

The Minister, in fact, must carry out the competent actions in accordance with EU law on the prevention and remedying of environmental damage, respecting the assignments of the Regions, the Autonomous Provinces and local public institutions, observing in particular the constitutional principles of subsidiarity and loyal cooperation.

For preliminary examination purposes, the Minister can use, also through special agreements, public and private persons known for their technical-scientific skills in the sector, within the limits of the administration's available resources.[182] Therefore, the norm examined identifies beforehand the person who can sue for the compensation of environmental damage, as per articles 311 et seq., Title III, of the Environmental Code, this person being the Minister of the Environment.

The Minister has the right to take legal action in ordinary criminal and/or civil proceedings, with the support of the State Attorney's offices,[183] or through an administrative procedure aimed at adopting the ordinance through which he orders those liable to reimburse the environmental damage, as per articles 312-316 of the Code.

These norms, as mentioned, are tied to articles 304 and 305 that govern prevention and restoration measures, this last definition being more in line with the competent administrative authority.

The aforesaid actions are alternatives since, if the Minister of the Environment «has adopted the ordinance referred to in Article 313, he can neither propose nor proceed further in the judgment for the compensation of the environmental damage, without prejudice to the possibility of taking action as a person damaged by the offense in a criminal legal action».[184]

If the Minister of the Environment chooses to commence

---

[182] See Environmental Code, art. 299, paragraphs II-IV.

[183] Pursuant to art. 311, paragraph I, «the Minister of the Environment and Protection of the Territory and Sea acts, also by exercising civil action in criminal proceedings, for the compensation of environmental damage in specific form and, if necessary, for the equivalent in assets, or proceeds as per the provisions of Part Six of this decree».

[184] See art. 315.

administrative proceedings, to be carried out as per Law 241/1990,[185] he must determine in advance the remedial measures to be implemented according to the criteria established in Annexes 3 and 4 to Part Six of the Environmental Code.[186]

Secondly, the previously mentioned administrative authority will proceed to identify the person liable for the environmental damage. In this regard, the Minister, for the purpose of presenting evidence «may delegate the Prefect competent for the territory and avail himself, through appropriate agreements, of the collaboration of the State's District attorneys, State Forestry Corps, Carabinieri, State Police, and Italian Finance Police and any other public body possessing adequate jurisdiction».[187]

Furthermore, in order to verify the facts, the Minister has the right to use technical consultants, to access for inspection purposes[188] and to ask judicial authorities for the authorization to carry out searches and seizures in the ways and within the limits prescribed by law.[189] These latter two powers of inspection, in addition to having to be expressly authorized by a judicial authority, can in any case be contested through appeals provided for by the special law under examination, i.e. Part Six of the Environmental Code. It is also assumed that the aforementioned activities be deferred to the competent Prefect or to police forces or to the other bodies mentioned above.

The ministerial ordinance, containing the requirements pursuant to art. 314, paragraphs I and II,[190] must be adopted within one hundred

---

[185] See the Environmental Code, art. 312, paragraph I. This provision is presumably also applicable to the ordinances referred to in Articles 304 and 305 of the Code.

[186] See art. 311, paragraph III.

[187] See art 312, paragraph II.

[188] See Law no. 241 of August 18, 1990, art. 6, paragraph I, lett. b).

[189] See the Environmental Code, art. 312, paragraphs III-VIII.

[190] In particular, the ministerial provision «contains the specific indication of the fact, commission or omission, contested, as well as of the elements of fact deemed relevant to identify and calculate the damage and the source of proof for the identification of the offenders [. . .] The order establishes a deadline, also agreed with the offender as applied in art. 11 of the law no. 241 of August 7, 1990, to restore the sites to their original state at his expense, in any case not less than two months and no more than two years, unless a further extension is determined in consideration of the entity of

and eighty days from when the operator is informed of the start of the preliminary activity, and in any case within two years from the notification of the damaging event, with the only exception being if environmental restoration is already underway at the expense and under the liability of the offender. In this case, the time period will start from the unjustified suspension of the restoration works, or from their conclusion if the remedy of damage was not completed.[191]

If the criminal court passed a sentence or a provision for the application of the sanction upon a request pursuant to art. 444 of the criminal code,[192] the judge's registry will send a copy of these rulings to the Minister of the Environment no later than five days from their publication. Furthermore, the Regions, the Autonomous Provinces and the local Public Institutions shall inform the Minister about the administrative sanctions within ten days of their issuance, so as to proceed with the environmental damage compensation.[193]

If the operator finds himself in financial difficulty, a ministerial ordinance and a judge's ruling may establish that payment be made in monthly installments, not exceeding twenty in number, and for an amount of not less than five thousand euros each. If the operator fails to pay even one installment on its due date, he will lose this benefit and will be forced to pay the rest of the entire sum due.

A debtor who requests to pay in installments is allowed to settle the debt incurred with one single payment at any time.[194]

---

the necessary works ... The ministerial orders referred to in articles 304, paragraph 3, and 313 indicate the remedy procedures and related terms».

[191] See Environmental Code, art. 313, paragraph IV.

[192] This is the so called "plea bargain". In particular, pursuant to paragraph I of art. 444 of the Criminal Code «the defendant and the public prosecutor can ask the judge to apply, in the case and to the extent indicated, an alternative sanction or a fine, reduced up to a third, or a custodial sentence when, keeping into account the circumstances and reduced up to one third, it will not exceed five years by itself or in conjunction with a financial penalty».

[193] See Environmental Code, art. 314, paragraphs IV and V.

[194] See art. 317, paragraphs II-IV.

Moreover, the Minister may issue further provisions towards liable parties identified afterwards, within the limitation period for compensation of damages deriving from an unlawful act as foreseen in art. 2947 of the Civil Code, paragraph I and III.

In particular, the right to compensation expires five years after the day in which the offense occurred. If the offense is subject to criminal sanctions, the time periods correspond to those established for the limitation period of the offense, with the same starting date, without prejudice to its occurred extinguishment, in which case the time period takes on a new limitation period within five years from the date of the offence's extinguishment.

In the event that compensation for damage has already occurred, additional charges to the person liable for the damage as a result of concurrent action by another authority other than the Minister are excluded.[195]

If, on the other hand, the enjoined operator does not carry out the remedy measures provided for in the ordinance, the Minister will re-order the operator to pay the sums corresponding to the costs of the measures that the intends to undertake.[196]

This last provision does not appear to comply with the articles 8.2 and 10 of Directive 2004/35/EC, according to which the competent authority can demand payment of the above sums only after taking measures to remedy the environmental damage. The Minister, in fact, has the right to undertake such measures with right of recourse against the operator, as confirmed by the aforementioned provisions of art. 305 of the code.

Within sixty days from notice, the offender may appeal against the order of immediate enforcement issued by the Minister[197] with the Regional Administrative Court (TAR), that is competent for the site in which environmental damage was caused, having the right to submit an opposition before the appeal, pursuant to art. 310, paragraph I and II.

---

[195] See Environmental Code, art. 313, paragraphs V-VII.
[196] See art. 313, paragraph II.
[197] See art. 313, paragraph I.

Also, in this case, this does not prejudice the right to extraordinarily petition to the President of the Republic within one hundred and twenty days of receiving the injunction or of becoming fully aware of its clauses.[198]

However, even in the case where the damage was caused by individuals subject to the exclusive jurisdiction of the Court of Auditors, the Minister is obliged to submit all the documentation to the Regional Office in the jurisdictional section of the Court competent for the territory, so that the procedure will be carried out before this same Court.[199]

The regulations on the prevention and remediation of environmental damage therefore confirm the transversal nature of the environment as an asset, the damage to which can be ascertained and calculated both by means of administrative procedures, which provide for the related legal guarantees, and through actions before an ordinary court, except for the exclusive jurisdiction of the special administrative judge in the cases established by law.

Lastly, the sums owed by the liable operator, including those deriving from the enforcement of guarantees taken on by him as a guarantee of compensation for environmental damage in favor of the State, shall be levied by the Minister pursuant to Legislative Decree no. 112 of April 13, 1999.

The aforementioned income, therefore, shall be «contributed into the State's accounts to be fully reassigned with a decree of the Minister of Economy and Finance to a relevant item of estimates of the Ministry of the Environment and Protection of the Territory and Sea, so as to be used to implement prevention and remedy measures in compliance with the provisions of Directive 2004/35/EC and with the obligations arising therefrom».[200]

---

[198] See Environmental Code, art. 316.
[199] See art. 313, paragraph VI.
[200] See art. 317, paragraphs I and VII.

72

This provision has replaced[201] the original paragraph V,[202] which provided for the sums collected by the competent authority to be placed into a "revolving fund" whose purpose was, in turn, to allocate the aforementioned revenues to the measures to be implemented for the prevention, reclamation and remedy or to scientific research activities.

Nevertheless, a clear conceptual reference to the fund exists in the section of article 317 of the code: *"Riscossione dei crediti e fondo di rotazione"* (*Debt collection and revolving fund*). The legislator's unclear intervention, furthermore, appears even more evident from the fact that letters a) - d) of the same paragraph, have no syntactical connection with the first replaced part. These letters, in particular, still show the various types of activities to which the sums collected and allocated as entries in the State budget should be assigned (no longer to the fund, as hoped for by the European Directive 2004/35/EC).

2.4 Criteria for the evaluation and remediation of damaged environmental components

Determining the compensation for environmental damage still presents problems of application and compliance with the provisions contained in the framework Directive 2004/35/EC on Environmental Liability, with regard to prevention and remedying of environmental damage.

As already mentioned, with an infringement procedure against Italy, the European Commission has contested the incompatibility of certain provisions relating to compensation for environmental damage contained in Part Six of the Environmental Code, as compared to the European legislation introduced with the aforementioned directive.

According to this regulation, in fact, the remedying of environmental damage can only take place in specific form. In particular, in Annex II of

---

[201] By virtue of art. 24 of the European Law 97/2013.

[202] Inspired in turn by art. 18, paragraph IX *bis* and *ter*, Law 349/1986.

this regulation, a distinction is made between damage to habitats, protected natural species and water, and damage to the soil.

In the first case, the remedying consists in restoring the damaged environment to its original conditions, by means of "primary" remedying, understood as any remedial measure that restores the damaged natural resources and/or services to or towards their original conditions; "complementary" remedying consists in any remedial measure undertaken in relation to natural resources and/or services aimed at offsetting a failure in completely restoring the damaged natural resources and or services; "compensatory" remedying, i.e. any action aimed at offsetting the temporary loss of natural resources and/or services from the date the environmental damage occurs to when the primary remedying is completed.

With regard to compensatory remedying, temporary losses mean losses resulting from the fact that damaged natural resources and/or services cannot perform their ecological functions or provide services to other natural resources or to the public until the primary or complementary measures are completed.

Only if primary remedying is not possible, should a complementary and/or compensatory remedying be implemented, the extent of which shall be determined according to the equivalent methods of resource-resource or service-service.

In particular, actions that provide natural resources and/or services of the same type, quality and quantity of those damaged shall be taken into consideration. In the event that such actions are not possible, alternative resources and/or services must be provided, possibly with the same value and function as the lost ones.

Where equivalent methods cannot be applied, alternative assessment methods should be used.

Specifically, the competent authority has the power to order the method to be used to determine the "extent" within which the complementary and compensatory measures can be applied, such as, for example, a monetary assessment. In this regard, the cost of the aforementioned measures corresponds to the estimated value of the lost ecological resources and services.[203]

In the case of damage to the soil, however, the remedying is conceived anthropically: it does not affect the natural resource as such, rather it has the object of removing any significant risks that are harmful to human health. The remedying shall be preceded by the completion of risk assessment procedures «which take into account the characteristics and function of the soil, the type and concentration of the substances, the harmful preparations, organisms or micro-organisms, the relative risks and possibility of their dispersion».

Once this operation is completed, measures must be taken to eliminate, limit or reduce the contaminants present in the soil, so that the natural resources shall not threaten human health in any way. Measures, however, have to take into account, where possible, the natural restoration of the damaged resource without any direct action by Man.[204]

Furthermore, differently from the green book and white book, the European Directive does not oblige the interested operators to be covered by insurance, not even for the exercise of intrinsically hazardous activities as defined in Annex III of the Directive. In Recital no. 27 of the document in question, the approval of such obligation by Member States is only hoped for but not imposed.

The same point also assumes the creation of a guarantee fund in insolvency situations or when there is a failure to identify the operator liable for environmental damage.

However, even this consideration is not supported by the provisions of art. 14, which broadly confers to Member States the obligation to guarantee «measures to encourage the development, by appropriate economic and financial operators, of financial guarantee tools and markets, including financial mechanisms in the event of insolvency, to allow operators to use financial guarantees to fulfill their responsibilities».

---

[203] See Directive 2004/35/EC, Annex II, par. I.
[204] See Annex II, par. 2.

Furthermore, in line with international practices, the polluter pays principle shall be implemented by excluding the liability of the Member States and, therefore, the latter's obligation to carry out remedial measures in the event of insolvency or non-identification of the operator liable for the environmental damage, that is provided for, instead, in the white book. Therefore, as for preventive measures, Member States only have a mere faculty to carry out the necessary remedial measures.

The European Directive, in any case, allows for the possibility of extending the cases in which it is not applied. This is in fact without prejudice to the possibility for Member States to approve stricter regulations on the prevention and remedying of environmental damage, including those to identify other professional activities and persons liable (including States) to be subject to the obligations established by the directive.[205]

Under Italian domestic law, the environmental code, in a first analysis, has used the same procedures as the directive to calculate and remedy environmental damage.

Even if Part Six's systematic approach suggests a distinction between restoration pursuant to art. 305 et seq. and environmental compensation as referred to in art. 311-316 of the code, these notions are actually equivalent.

Remedying the environmental damage is the important aspect, that is returning the damaged natural resources or services back to their original conditions, with the exception of damage to the soil, in which case the removal of risks of harmful effects for the environment and human health is sufficient.[206]

The provision of art. 298 *bis*, paragraph II, states that the remedying of damage to natural resources has to be implemented according to the rules established in Title II, that is for the prevention and restoration of the environment, and in Annex 3 to Part Six, to

---

[205] See Directive 2004/35 / EC, recital no. 29 and arts. 3.2 and 16.1.
[206] See the Environmental Code, art. 302, paragraph IX and attachment 3, paragraph I.

which also art. 311 paragraph II, Title III of the code refers to, with regard to compensatory actions for environmental damage.

Therefore, the primary, complementary and compensatory remedying procedures referred to in the European Directive were resumed, with regard to the services of natural resources that were lost or temporarily damaged and with the same distinction as for the soil contamination.[207]

Furthermore, to determine the aforementioned remedying measures, the criteria adopted will be those established by the resource-resource, service-service directive and, in a lesser way, other criteria, among which a financial assessment only to determine the extent of the complementary and compensatory measures.[208] As for damage to the soil, the same measures will be considered for the removal of any contaminating agent that could affect human health, subject to prior risk assessment activities.[209]

However, with the deletion of letter i), of art. 303, by the 2013 European law, the provisions pertaining to the contamination of this last natural resource cannot be distinguished from those relating to the reclamation referred to in articles. 239 et seq., Part Four, of the Environmental Code, having as its object «the series of measures aimed at eliminating pollution sources and polluting substances or reducing their concentrations into the soil, the subsoil and in groundwater at a level equal to or lower than the values of the risk threshold concentrations (CSR)».[210]

In this regard, the new article 298 *bis* introduced by this law, under paragraph III defines only systems applicable to the soil, subsoil and groundwater contamination which took place before the European law or the Code came into force, according to specific conditions:

---

[207] See Directive 2004/35/EC, Annex 3, paragraph I lett. a) to d).

[208] See Annex 3, paragraph I, par. 1.2.

[209] See Annex 3, paragraph I, par. 2.

[210] Environmental Code, Part Four, art. 240, paragraph I, lett. p).

Title V of Part Four of this Legislative Decree regulates the soil and subsoil restoration measures planned and implemented in compliance with the principles and criteria established under point 2 of Annex 3 to Part Six, as well as the groundwater remedying measures planned and implemented in compliance with point 1 of Annex 3; or, for pollution prior to April 29, 2006, the remedying measures of groundwater that achieve the quality objectives within the time limits established by Part Three of this decree.

With regard to pollution occurring after the 2013 reform, the criteria for the application of the different legislations on reclamation and compensation of environmental damage pertaining to the soil, are not defined.

This overlapping, therefore, generates considerable problems, since norms regarding reclamation have a retroactive effect, provide solely for a regime of culpable liability (attributable only to the "person liable") and that inquiries and decision-making powers be left to the Regions and local authorities.[211]

Furthermore, despite the corrections made first with Law Decree no. 135 of 2009[212] and most recently with European Law no. 97 of 2013, various provisions of the code regarding compensation for environmental damage are still conflicting and refer to the remedying in financial terms, that is, based on equivalent assets.

The above-mentioned provisions, therefore, are incompatible with the Directive 2004/35/EC, to the point that a future and additional infringement procedure against Italy is not to be excluded.[213]

First of all, art. 311 of the code, the initial norm of Title III regarding compensation for environmental damage, although classified as *Specific Compensation Action*, in the same first paragraph states that «the Minister of the Environment and Protection of the Territory and the Sea

---

[211] See Environmental Code, art. 242.

[212] Converted into Law no. 166 of 2009.

[213] For a further analysis on the subject, please refer to F. Boscolo *Il risarcimento del danno ambientale. Profili di analisi*, (Compensation for environmental damage. Analysis), CLEUP, 2015.

acts, also exercising civil action in criminal proceedings, to specifically compensate the environmental damage and, if necessary, based on equivalent assets».

Although law 97/2013 has removed the phrase "based on equivalent assets" from the article's heading, a conceptual reference of the provision examined continues in the text, probably due to an oversight of the legislator.

Another similar oversight can be found in art. 313, paragraph II, which states that if the liable party fails to adopt remedial measures, the Minister of the Environment will determine the sum necessary to undertake said measures and re-order their payment. Although the order is functional to the subsequent adoption of the remedial measures for the environmental damage to be carried out by the Minister, this provision contradicts what established by art. 10 and by Annex II of the European directive.

The competent authority is entitled to collect the sums corresponding to the cost of the aforementioned measures only after undertaking them, to guarantee that the remediation of the damaged environmental media has actually taken place.

In this regard, the provision of art. 298 *bis*, paragraph II also does not appear to be compliant, which allows the remaining remediation to be implemented «where necessary, also by carrying out procedures aimed at obtaining from the person who caused the damage, or the imminent threat of it, the resources necessary to cover the costs of the remediation measures to be adopted and that have not been implemented by that person».

In any case, the criteria and methods of monetary assessment to determine the extent of the complementary and compensatory remedial measures, which the Minister should have already established with a decree, as per paragraph III of art. 311, are still uncertain.

Also controversial is the provision of art. 313, paragraph VI, according to which in the event of damage caused by individuals who are subject to the exclusive jurisdiction of the Court of Auditors, the Minister of the Environment, «Instead of ordering a damage payment based on equivalent assets, a report will be sent to the Regional Public Prosecutor's Office at the jurisdictional section of the Court of Auditors competent for the territory».

Furthermore, the previously mentioned art. 306 *bis*, paragraph II, lett. c) even allows, although in a residual way and limited to damage to sites of national interest, a negotiation between the operator and the competent authority concerning the settlement of the aforementioned damage in monetary terms, therefore, based on equivalent assets.

Lastly, the provision pursuant to art. 314 should be considered, based on which – according to the Minister's order - the calculation of environmental damage should include both damage to the natural resource and the cost necessary for its recovery, without however providing any clear criteria to determine this, also not being in line with the European legislator.

Therefore, the environmental damage shall be remedied by restoring the compromised natural resources and/or services to their conditions prior to contamination, except for damage to the soil, for which it will be enough to eliminate the risk of harmful effects for human health.

Damage will be calculated based on resource-resource and service-service criteria, and where these cannot be applied, alternative criteria will be adopted such as value-cost, i.e. a financial evaluation, to determine only the extent of the remedial measures.

It follows that compensation based on equivalent assets in a strict sense is to be excluded, also due to the difficulty in determining this.

However, similar to the directive, there shall be no other penalties in addition to the obligation of remedying the damaged environmental media, which could well be imposed to further discourage (and thus prevent) the production of the aforementioned damages.

The environmental code provides for financial administrative fines only in the case of delay, by the operator, in the implementation of prevention/restoration measures or in informing the competent authority of the environmental damage or threat of it.

Therefore, there are no provisions to apply these fines in addition to the aforesaid measures.

The same applies to administrative bans, such as, for example, the revocation of an administrative provision authorizing the exercise of the polluting activity.[214]

In fact, financial sanctions and bans can only be imposed by an ordinary criminal court in the event of conviction for environmental crimes pursuant to art. 25 *undecies* of Legislative Decree no. 231 of 2001.[215]

In particular, the aforesaid judicial authority, in the event of an offense of environmental disaster or pollution, has the right to apply either a financial fine or one of the following bans: exclusion from facilitations, financing and subsidies, or revocation of those already granted; prohibition to advertise products or services; prohibition to stipulate contracts with the Public Administration; suspension or revocation of authorizations, licenses or concessions; ban from exercising an activity.

Therefore, the Minister of the Environment cannot apply the same sanctions in alternative to the criminal court.[216] The administrative action, among other things, is carried out through simplified procedures

---

[214] Bans are based on art. 20 of Law 689/1981: «The administrative authority with an order-injunction or the criminal court with a sentence of conviction as provided in Article 24, may apply, as administrative sanctions, those provided in the applicable laws, for individual violations, as criminal penalties, when they consist in the deprivation or suspension of faculties and rights deriving from administrative procedures». These sanctions are ancillary, with purely punitive purposes: they involve the deprivation or suspension of faculties or benefits granted by an administrative measure.

[215] On the legislation regarding the «administrative liability of companies and bodies» deriving from an offense. Art. 25 *undecies*, registered as Environmental crimes, was introduced by art. 2, Legislative Decree. no. 121 of 2011, and subsequently amended by art. 1, paragraph VIII, Law no. 68 of 2015.

[216] The joint application of the same sanctions by both administrative and judicial authorities is certainly to be excluded as it would violate the prohibition of a double proceeding, the so called *ne bis in idem* proceeding, established in the Italian legal system.

of a shorter duration with respect to proceedings before the aforementioned judicial authority.

On this point, it is useful to refer to the Constitutional Court's judgment, no. 49 of 2015:

one must be aware that the separation of an administrative offense from criminal law, in addition to obliging the legislator to use great discretion in identifying the most effective tools to pursue the «Effectiveness in imposing obligations or duties» [. . .] also corresponds, in terms of constitutional guarantees, to the «principle of subsidiarity, for which criminalization, which constitutes the last resort, must intervene only when other branches of the law do not offer adequate protection to the assets that need to be secured» [. . .] In fact, the «Constitutional protection requirements do not end [. . .] with a (possible) criminal protection, but can be met with different forms of precepts and of [. . .] It is in fact a consolidated principle that 'punishment' can also be applied by an administrative authority, albeit on condition that the decision can be challenged before a court which offers the guarantees included in art. 6 of the ECHR, but which does not necessarily exercise criminal jurisdiction».

Furthermore, with particular reference to the restrictive sanction of seizure,[217] the judgment adds that «the administrative sanctioning power, to which such measure is assigned before the possible intervention of the criminal court judge, relates well to the public interest of the 'territory's building plan' [. . .] for which the public administration is responsible. An interest, it is worthwhile noting, which is not in fact unrelated to the future developments of the ECHR (judgment of November 8, 2005, Saliba vs. Malta)».

With reference to the authority of an ordinary civil judge, there is no provision for the latter to condemn (always alternatively to the administrative authority or the criminal court) the operator for the so-called "punitive damages"[218] of an Anglo-Saxon origin.

This refers to the condemnation of the author of the harmful incident to pay a sum of money in addition to damage compensation, when the

---

[217] See Law no. 689 of 1981, art. 20, paragraph III, IV and V.
[218] From English Punitive damages.

action or omission related to it is committed with intent or gross negligence

In the Italian legal system, the aforementioned damages have been exceptionally approved. An example of this is art. 96 of the Italian Civil Code, paragraph I, with the combined provisions of paragraph III, introduced by art. 45, paragraph XII, Law no. 69, of June 18, 2009. In particular, when established that the losing party has acted wrongfully or resisted in bad faith or has been negligent (gross negligence - not excusable, to be assessed according to the circumstances of the case),[219] the judge «in any case, when deciding on the expenditure according to article 91 [. . .] also of his own motion, may also order the losing party to pay, in favor of the other party, a sum equitably determined».[220]

Although the sum is intended to be paid to a party in the proceedings, rather than to the State, the caselaw of the Supreme Court has recognized the essential purpose of public authority power and the deterrent nature of the aforementioned sanction, since conduct aimed at exploiting the trial would cause «an unjust aggravation of the juridical system, provoking a useless waste of time and energy on this system».[221]

In environmental matters, art. 18, paragraph VI of Law 349/1986, although referring to compensation based on equivalent assets, provides the civil court with the possibility to settle the environmental damage in terms of both compensation and sanctions,[222] also considering the degree of guilt and severity of fraud of the person liable: «where a precise quantification of the damage is not possible, the judge determines the amount in an equitable manner, taking into account the gravity of the

---

[219] See Code of Civil Procedure, art. 96, paragraph I.

[220] See art. 96, paragraph III.

[221] Supreme Court (*Corte di Cassazione*), judgment no. 3376 of 2016. Of a different viewpoint C. Asprella, *L'art 96, comma 3, c.p.c. tra danni punitivi e funzione indennitaria*, (art. 96, paragraph 3, Civ. Proc. Code between punitive damage and indemnity function), in Corr. Giur., 2016.

[222] In this sense, see L. Bigliazzi Geri, *A proposito di danno ambientale ex art. 18 Law of July 8, 1986, no. 349 e di Responsabilità civile*, in Politica del diritto, 1987, p. 257.

individual fault, the costs necessary for the restoration and the profit achieved by the offender as a consequence of his detrimental behavior to the environmental assets».

The aforementioned early provision, however, was repealed by art. 318, paragraph II, lett. a), of the Environmental Code, and was never even resumed in the original text[223] of art. 311, which in paragraph II and III referred to various notions expressed in art. 18 of Law 349/1986.

The controversial[224] category of punitive damages is legitimately justified at a European level in Regulation no. 864 of 2007, which under Recital no. 32 excludes the admissibility of the aforementioned damages in contrast with the internal public order only if they are excessive:

the application of a legal provision defined by this regulation to determine non-compensatory damages of an exemplary or excessively punitive nature can be considered contrary to the public policy of the court, considering the circumstances of the present case in question of the legal system of the Member State's court.

In this regard, the first section of the Civil Supreme Court (*Corte di Cassazione*) also recently ruled in favor, with order no. 9978 of 2016, referring the decision of admissibility of *punitive damages* in Italy to the Supreme Court's United Sections, acknowledging a United States judgment.
In particular, according to one of the parties involved, the American provision called for a punishment for *punitive damages*, which is

---

[223] Before the modification made by the European Law 97/2013.

[224] See Supreme Court (*Corte di Cassazione*), judgment no. 1183 of 2007. Among the authors, reluctant to introduce punitive damages into the Italian legal system, C.M. Bianca, *Diritto civile. V. La responsabilità* Milano, 2012; G. Scarselli, *Il nuovo art. 96, 3° comma, c.p.c.: consigli per l'uso*, in Foro it. 2010.

typical in Anglo-Saxon *Common law*,[225] but is not admissible in the Italian legal system, being contrary to public policy, as confirmed by the Supreme Court.[226]

In this circumstance, the referring section expressed the need to have the civil liability system evolve into a multi-functional one (no longer solely compensatory, but also with sanctions and deterrents), which also takes into account the modern need to harmonize legal systems both on an international and European level.

This orientation - stated the first section of the Court - was already expressed with the previous judgment no. 7613 of 2015, which considered the incompatibility between the legal system in question and the public policy to be unfounded. As proof of this, it has also been shown by caselaw how in reality the polyvalent compensation-affliction-deterrence nature of civil liability, especially with regard to damage to the juridical system, had already been considered when the civil code was drawn up.

Moreover, according to this section, the previously mentioned polyvalence is supported by the introduction into the Italian legal system of other types of compensation also having a sanctioning and deterrent function, particularly in the field of industrial property, defamation by the press and civil procedure liability.

The United Sections of the Supreme Court (*Corte di Cassazione*), with judgment no. 16601 of 2017, put an end to all disputes, accepting the

---

[225] From English, "common law", i.e. unwritten customary law. The Anglo-Saxon Common law legal systems are based above all on the so-called "rules of precedent", instead of statute law, as occurs in the so-called Civil law of Roman legal systems.

[226] See Supreme Court (*Corte di Cassazione*), judgment no. 1183 of 2007. On this point, see L. Nivarra, *Brevi considerazioni a margine dell'ordinanza di remissione alle Sezioni Unite sui "danni punitivi"*, in Contemporary Civil Accounting Law, January 30, 2017; M. Schirippa, *I danni punitivi nel panorama internazionale e nella situazione italiana: verso il loro riconoscimento?*, in www.comparazionedirittocivile.it, March 2017; M. Grondona, *L'auspicabile "via libera" ai danni punitivi, il dubbio limite del- l'ordine pubblico e la politica del diritto di matrice giurisprudenziale (a proposito del dialogo tra ordinamenti e giurisdizioni)*, in Contemporary Civil Law, 31st July 2016.

definitive introduction of punitive damages into the Italian legal system, declaring the following principle of law:

In the current legal system, civil liability does not only have the task of restoring assets to the person suffering the damage, but the system also includes deterrent and sanctioning functions of the person civilly liable.
The system of punitive damages of US origin is therefore not ontologically incompatible with the Italian legal system.
The acknowledgement of a foreign judgment containing a ruling of this type must however correspond to the condition that it was given in the foreign legal system based on norms guaranteeing the tradition of this type of conviction, its predictability and quantitative limits, only considering, during its enforcement, the effects of the foreign judgment and their compatibility with the public policy.

Therefore, the regulations on the prevention and remediation of environmental damage can again be conceived as a sanction, as originally provided for in the repealed art. 18, paragraph VI, of Law no. 349 of 1986, aimed at encouraging the prevention of damages, that are sometimes irreversible, such as those made to natural media.

Evidently this is irrespective to the fact that Italian law refers to, or better, should refer only to compensation in a specific form, rather than for equivalent assets, of the environmental damage.

The European Directive 2004/35/EC itself, as noted, stresses that the key "polluter pays principle" of the environmental liability must guarantee the real remediation of the ecological damage and at the same time discourage the production of similar damage by the operators.[227]

In this regard, according to Recital 29, as well as to articles 3.2 and 16 of the Directive, this shall be without prejudice to any further European legislation governing the exercise of one of the activities falling within its scope and to the national rules that extend environmental liability to

---

[227] See Directive 2004/35/EC, recital no. 2.

other persons, as well as those related to the prevention and remediation of environmental damage that are stricter and more restrictive.

Accordingly, interim injunctions are not yet explicitly recognized with regard to the protection of the natural resources considered *per se*, but only aim at protecting the owner's subjective right to a sound environment. In fact, the competent authority cannot order nor judicially obtain the precautionary suspension of harmful emissions produced by the professional activity carried out by the identified operator.

The State is not liable in any way, and therefore does not have the burden of acting in the event of insolvency or failure of identifying (through administrative or legal proceedings) the person liable for the environmental damage or the threat of it, even if foreseen in the preparatory work for Directive 2004/35/EC, particularly in the White Paper.

The Minister of the Environment, in fact, "has the power" to adopt measures to prevent, contain and remedy/restore the environment. Furthermore, while only a couple of articles are dedicated to the precaution and prevention of ecological damage, many norms contained in Part Six of the code, including the entire Annex 3, refer to its remedying. The prevention of this damage, in particular, could be increased by adequate provisions for sanctions, rewards for virtuous operators, and economic incentives for eco-production.

Lastly, it should be noticed that there is no obligation to stipulate insurance policies for the operators concerned, not even for the exercise of professional activities deemed dangerous, although this is suggested in the European directive.

The only financial guarantee provided for in the Environmental Code is the specific chapter on the State budget, which has also replaced the revolving fund referred to in the European provisions, into which the income deriving from the recovery of the costs for the adoption of precautionary, prevention and remedial measures of environmental damage should flow.

Chapter III

SPECIAL CASES OF ENVIRONMENTAL LIABILITY

3.1. The liability of the owner or operator of the damaged area

The regulations on the prevention and remediation of environmental damage defined in the Environmental Code to implement the obligation of result established by Directive no. 2004/35/EC, is a special law, introduced in the Italian legal system to specifically regulate the cases of liability for damage to the environment.

To this end, art. 298 *bis*, paragraph I, of the Code, introduced by art. 25, paragraph I, of the European law no. 97 of 2013 gives a clear indication, and based on what is provided in art. 3.1 of the European directive, establishes that

legislation contained in Part Six of the present legislative decree applies to:

a) environmental damage caused by any one of the professional activities listed in Annex 5 to Part Six and to any imminent threat of such damage resulting from the aforementioned activities;

b) environmental damage caused by activities other than those listed in Annex 5 of Part Six and to any imminent threat of such damage deriving from the aforesaid activities, in case of fraud or negligent behavior.

As a rule, therefore, the aforementioned legislation can be neither integrated nor waived from the norms of the civil code.

However, as known, statute law is not always able to cover all specific cases. Therefore, the legislation on environmental liability at times also shows its limits when particular cases occur which question the applicability of this legislation.

Waste disposal, for example, is already a dangerous activity in itself, and can give rise to a mixture of forms of liability and, therefore, of legislations, regarding both the Environmental and Civil Codes.

This is possible, upon a first analysis, because the person liable for pollution may also be the owner or manager of the polluted land, who, due to the questionable removal of letter i), of art. 303, of the Environmental Code, could be obliged, in addition to removing the waste (articles 192 et. seq.), to also implement reclamation (articles 239 et. seq.) and remedy the damage to the soil (articles 298 *bis* and et. seq.).

The European Directive itself, in Recital no. 29, does not prevent Member States «to adopt appropriate provisions in situations where a double recovery of costs might result due to concurrent action by competent authorities in accordance with this Directive».

Secondly, on the other hand, the owner/operator of the area contaminated by third parties could be held liable for the propagation of pollution towards other sites.

This case is not considered either in the European Directive or in the Environmental Code, leaving doubts therefore on the applicability of the environmental legislation and the possibility of integrating it with the norms contained in the Civil Code.

As noted, the European Directive, in Recital no. 13, indicates the need to identify polluters for the purpose of applying this regulation, as well as the importance of the existence of a causal link between their activities and the environmental damage, which has to be, inter alia, concrete and quantifiable.

This consideration was also supported by the European Court of Justice, which, with the historical judgment C-378/08 of 2010, interpreted the polluter pays principle, and confirmed the attributing the environmental liability, both objective as unintentional, solely to the identified operator, upon detection of the causal link.

In particular, the existence of this link can be presumed on the basis of the proximity between the operator's activity and the contaminated area, and (jointly) to the type of materials used by him in his production processes and the polluting agents detected on the damaged site.[228]

---

[228] This interpretation was confirmed by the EU Court of Justice with the subsequent ruling of 4 March 2015 - case c-534/13.

Nevertheless, with regard to the owner/operator of the damaged site, nothing is specified with regard to his either being not guilty or his possible involvement in the environmental liability.

The Directive and Part Six of the code, in fact, only provides that the competent authority (the Minister) urge the persons entitled to request his action and the persons on whose lands the remedial measures should be made to submit their observations, taking them therefore into consideration.[229]

In truth, Part Four of the Environmental Code, covering the subject of reclamation of polluted sites, is the part that regulates, first of all, the position of the owner or manager of the area polluted by third parties.

Pursuant to art. 245, paragraph II, of the code, if the guiltless owner/operator finds that the threshold of the maximum allowable exposure limits (EL) on the site is exceeded or that there is a real and concrete danger of exceeding these limits, the owner/operator shall immediately notify the competent authorities and shall implement preventive measures according to the procedures set out under previous art. 242.

The competent authority shall therefore seek to identify the person liable so as to ensure that the foreseen reclamation procedures are carried out, without prejudice to the right of the area owner or operator to undertake the reclamation measures himself on his own property.

The latter person, therefore, does not have any obligation to carry out reclamation on the area, being only required to give notice to the competent authority and perform any action to prevent damage, as defined by art. 304, Part Six, of the Environmental Code.

This was also explicitly confirmed by the State Council, according to which the guiltless owner or operator is only required to implement the necessary preventive measures,[230] in particular all «the initiatives to counter an event, an act or an omission that has created an imminent threat to health or the environment understood as a risk likely to result in

---

[229] See Directive 2004/35/EC, art. 7.4.; Environmental Code, art. 306, paragraph V.
[230] See State Council, judgment no. 4647 of 2016; no.550 of 2016.

health or environmental damage in the near future, in order to prevent or minimize the occurrence of this threat».[231]

Moreover, administrative judges have ruled out imposing reclamation obligations to the owner/operator of the damaged site for the mere fact of being that, thereby eradicating the so-called "Liability by virtue of one's position" (without guilt and causal link).

In particular, the provision referred to in art. 2051 of the Civil Code, i.e. the liability for «damage caused by something in custody» is not applicable to the case under examination. This is because the legislation defined in Part Four of the Environmental Code for the reclamation of contaminated sites is of a special nature with respect to the provisions of the Civil Code and considers the specific position of the guiltless owner/operator, and only applies to the persona liable of pollution as a result of willful misconduct or negligence.[232]

However, the execution of reclamation procedures by the competent authorities constitutes a charge[233] on the polluted property.

The authorities will therefore have a specific preferential right on the property,[234] being able to exercise a right of recourse against the property (even if it is sold to third parties) if the person liable is not identified or cannot reimburse the costs of the reclamation.

More specifically, art. 253 of the Environmental Code, states:

---

[231] State Council, judgment no. 4225 of 2015. Previously, the Regional Administrative Court of Lazio, had ruled to the contrary with judgment no. 2509 of 2015.

[232] See Regional Administrative Court of Friuli Venezia Giulia, judgment no. 183 of 2014; Regional Administrative Court of Tuscany, judgment no. 1664 of 2012. See, F. Anastasi, *La gestione dei siti inquinati: la responsabilità dell'inquinamento nella sentenza del TAR Lombardia n. 1326/2017*, (The management of polluted sites: liability for pollution in TAR Lumbardy's judgment no. 1326/2017) in "Rivista Giuridica Lexambiente" of 20 July 2017.

[233] It is an activity that concerns giving or doing, a charge that affects the holder of a fund for the fact of benefiting from the asset itself.

[234] A preferential right is the right of a creditor to be preferred based on the same conditions as other creditors. Preferential rights are based on the law. They are defined as specific preferential rights on the property since the guarantee that the right attributes to the creditor concerns a debtor's specific and "bound" real estate property. A creditor with a specific preferential right on a property as a rule also has preference over mortgage creditors.

The actions undertaken under this paragraph constitute a charge on the polluted sites if they are carried out as per law provisions by the competent authority pursuant to Article 250. The charge is entered following the approval of the reclamation project and shall be indicated in the town planning use certificate.

The expenses incurred for the measures referred to in paragraph I benefit from a preferential right on the same areas, pursuant to and for the purposes of article 2748, second paragraph, of the Italian Civil Code. Such right can also be applied with prejudice to the acquired rights by third parties on the real estate property.

The preferential right and recovery of expenses may be exercised against the guiltless owner of the site regarding pollution or the danger of pollution only following a substantiated decision by the competent authority justifying, among other things, the impossibility of verifying the identity of the liable person, that is the impossibility of exercising a right of recourse against this person or its uselessness.

In any case, an owner who is not liable for the pollution may be required to reimburse, on grounds of a substantiated provision and in compliance with the provisions of law no. 241 of August 7, the costs of the measures undertaken by the competent authority only within the limits of the market value of the site, determined following the execution of these measures. When an owner not liable for the pollution has spontaneously provided for the reclamation of the polluted site, he shall have a right of recourse against the person liable for the pollution for the costs incurred and for any greater damage suffered.

It should be noted that the competent authorities, that is the Municipality in which the contaminated site is located or, in the absence of this, the Region within which the Municipality is located, must carry out the reclamation procedures if the polluters are not identifiable, or neither they nor the owner of the polluted area voluntarily provide for this.[235]

Therefore, the structural differences with the liability system for environmental damage outlined in Part Six of the Environmental Code are evident, which, except for definitional fallacies, attributes the aforementioned liability to the "operator" and does not foresee the burden of the measure to be imposed upon the competent authority, identified as the Minister of the Environment.

---

[235] See the Environmental Code, art. 250.

The owner or operator of the contaminated site who has not voluntarily provided for the reclamation, therefore, may be subject to a recourse action by the administration, to recover the expenses incurred with this activity, also having a specific preferential right on the area and being preferred to mortgage creditors, pursuant to art. 2748 of the Civil Code, paragraph II.

In this case, not having a direct right of recourse against the person liable for pollution, the only remedy the aforementioned owner or operator will have is that of a compensatory action for non-contractual liability as per art. 2043 of the Civil Code, having therefore to prove the illegal event and the injustice of the damage suffered.

In the event that the contaminated property is transferred to third parties, the latter can exercise a right of recourse against the seller through a warranty action for defects of the property (article 1490 of the Italian Civil Code et. seq.), a damage compensation action for the sale of an asset totally different from the one agreed upon (articles 1490 of the Italian Civil Code and et. seq., 1497 of the Italian Civil Code, article 129, Leg. Decree 206/2005) and an action of invalidity of the sale for failure to attach the town planning use certificate (articles 1418 of the Italian Civil Code et. seq., article 40, paragraph II, Law 47/1985).[236]

Another hypothesis, however, is that in which there is a diffusion of pollution from the polluted site of the guiltless owner/operator towards other sites.

Given that neither the European directive nor the Environmental Code provide for anything in this respect, except for the obligations of prevention and notice by the aforementioned person, in light of this shortcoming, a part of case law[237] has endorsed the possibility of exceptionally integrating the environmental legislation with the aforementioned case referred to in art. 2051 of the Italian Civil Code.

---

[236] Refer to G. Inzaghi, R. Serrato, *Se il proprietario è incolpevole non deve bonificare*, (If the owner is guiltless, he has no reclamation obligation) in Sviluppo e Territorio, November 18th, 2015.

[237] See the Court of Venice, judgment no. 304/2010; Supreme Court (Corte di Cassazione), judgment no. 12329/2004.

In particular, according to this provision, «everyone is liable for the damage caused by the items held in safe custody, unless he proves the event was accidental (force majeure)».

This article, evidently, establishes a presumed liability of the person holding the items in custody, reversing the releasing burden of proof of the force majeure event on this person. This is an extremely rigorous burden of proof, since it is aimed at demonstrating unforeseen or unforeseeable external circumstances that would interrupt the causal link, or the existence of a third-party representation.

The person holding the item in custody, i.e. the person who has material access to the item (therefore not only the owner), has the legal obligation to monitor it constantly by adopting all measures necessary to prevent it from causing damage.

However, such person shall be exempt from civil liability for damages caused by the item held in custody only if he proves that, despite the implementation of the necessary precautionary measures, the damage was caused by unforeseeable or unforeseen external circumstances, or by a third party.

Therefore, the person who holds the item in safe custody shall take on the risk that such item might cause damage regardless of force majeure.

For a good part of case law and literature, art. 2051 of the Italian Civil Code constitutes a form of strict liability since, on one hand the person holding the item in custody is presumed to be civilly liable for the existence of a merely etiological link between the item held in custody and the damage caused by it; on the other hand, rigorous and positive proof is required, to which this person is bound, for the exemption of liability represented by force majeure, which is therefore considered a so-called *probatio diabolica*.[238]

In view of these considerations, regarding the position of the

---

[238] See G. Alpa, R. Garofoli, *Manuale di diritto civile*, Nel Diritto Editore, 2015; S. Camonita, *La responsabilità di cose in custodia*, in Filodiritto, February 4 2012. In case law, See Supreme Court (Corte di Cassazione), judgments no. 2660/2013; 11695/2009; 2563/2007; 376/2005; 12329/2004.

owner or of the person holding the site in safe custody, part of case law stated that the owner or the person holding the site in safe custody cannot have measures and acts applied against him, that are not attributable to the normal notion of supervision or control[239] insofar as these relate to the state of the asset, its economic use and any other circumstance.

Consequently, the liability for damage stemming from an item held in custody cannot be attributed to the owner or operator if he provides proof that he could not prevent the spreading of pollution and was not in the condition to physically watch over the site he held in custody, for reasons not depending on him.

This circumstance may occur, for example, in the case where the area in his custody is too widely extended to be constantly monitored, or when supervision requires a series of activities and operations that the owner/custodian cannot perform or support by himself.[240]

Under these circumstances, therefore, the liability for the spreading of pollution will be attributed only to the person who originally started it.

At a closer look therefore, the liability pursuant to art. 2051 of the Italian Civil Code of the owner or custodian of the area from which pollution has spread to other sites must be scrupulously verified by the judge according to the circumstances and to the specific case.

This is because the exceptional integration of art. 2051 of the Italian Civil Code, being a special regulation, cannot however oppose the principles of the Environmental Code, giving rise to a form of liability by virtue of the owner/custodian's position without even taking into account the minimum criteria for detecting a causal link, as established by the EU Court of Justice.

---

[239] See Supreme Court (Corte di Cassazione), judgment no. 7411/199; n. 4124/1975. To the contrary, see Supreme Court (Corte di Cassazione), judgment no. 10649/2004.
[240] In this regard, L. Prati, *Responsabilità per danno all'ambiente e bonifica dei siti contaminati*, (Liability for environmental damage and reclamation of contaminated sites), IPSOA Wolters Kluwer Group, Milanofiori Assago (MI), 2011.

3.2. The case of a plurality of liable parties causing an ecological damage

In the context of the regulations on the prevention and remediation of environmental damage, this analysis should also consider the case in which more than one person contributes to determining the environmental damage, in an active or omitting form. This often occurs currently; therefore, this case has its own specific regulations within the specific environmental legislation.

Recital no. 22 of Directive 2004/35/EC provides that «Member States may establish national rules defining the allocation of costs in the case of a plurality of perpetrators».

Article 9 of the Directive expressly states that such Directive «is without prejudice to any national law provision concerning cost allocation in the case of multiple damage perpetrators, in particular with regard to the division of liability between the producer and user of a product».

In the Italian legal system, the criteria of attributing liability to several persons who cause an ecological damage, has undergone radical changes.

The legislation prior to the approval of the European Directive and to the entry into force of the Environmental Code, established a liability of an individual-partial type for those who are accomplices in the same event of environmental damage, obliging the judge to take into account the extent of guilt and profit that was derived in causing the damaging event.

In fact, art. 18 of law no. 349 of 1986 established that:

Where a precise quantification of the damage is not possible, the judge shall determine the amount in an equitable manner, keeping into account the severity of the individual fault, the costs necessary for the restoration and the profit gained by the offender as a result of his detrimental behavior to the environmental assets.
In the event of having accomplices in the same damaging event, each

person will be charged according to his individual liability.[241]

Subsequently, art. 318 of the Environmental Code revoked the aforementioned article, with the exception of paragraph V, and not having expressly declared anything in that regard, it allowed for the exceptional integration of Article 2055 of the Italian Civil Code, which under the non-contractual heading attributes a joint and several liability to the offenders, unless otherwise determined.[242]

Lastly, with subsequent corrective measures,[243] the Italian legislator made changes to paragraph III of art. 311 of the Environmental Code, according to which «in the cases where accomplices are involved in the same damaging event, each of them shall be charged within the limits of his personal liability. The relative debt is transferred, according to the laws in force, to his heirs, within the limits of their actual profit».

These changes, therefore, have reintroduced a several liability, as provided for in the previously mentioned article 18. It follows that ascertaining the "personal liability" of the operators involved in causing the environmental damage cannot be separated from the existence of a subjective element of guilt, that is their willful misconduct or negligence.

As known, in criminal law, the concept of personal liability has been defined as the typical liability of an individual, that is one requiring a subjective reprimand and where the willful misconduct (volition-intention) or at least the guilt (negligence, imprudence, malpractice or

---

[241] Law no. 349 of 1986, art. 18, paragraphs VI and VII.
[242] Pursuant to art. 2055 of the Civil Code «if the damaging fact is attributable to more than one person, all are jointly and severally liable for damages. The one who has compensated the damage has recourse against each of the others, to the extent determined by the gravity of the respective guilt and the entity of the consequences that derive from it. In doubt, the individual faults are presumed equal». Similarly, in the context of contractual liability, art. 1294 of the Italian Civil Code establishes that «the co-debtors are jointly liable, if the law or title do not establish otherwise».
[243] See. L. no. 166/2009 and European Law no. 97/2013.

violation of rules of conduct) of the agent has been identified.[244]

Furthermore, the EU Court of Justice has recently ruled, confirming that

the remedying obligation lies with the operators only to an extent corresponding to their contribution in causing the pollution or risk of pollution. Therefore, the opposing theory of the administration cannot be shared, which considers joint and several liability to be more suitable for the protection of the public interest, aimed at guaranteeing a rapid action to secure the asset, without prejudice to the action of recourse against other liable parties, assuming that, due to the specific nature of the subject, the civil law principles regarding being accomplices to causing the damage - that impose the obligation of a joint compensation (Article 2055 of the Civil Code) - are not applicable.[245]

Nevertheless, the additional provision of art. 311, paragraph III, of the Environmental Code, does not seem to take into account the fact that the European law of 2013 introduced, under paragraph II, the strict liability for environmental damage caused by dangerous activities pursuant to Annex 5, which is incompatible with the provision examined.[246]

Furthermore, the questionable article 306 *bis* concerning a possible settlement between the Minister of the Environment and the operator responsible for the damage to the sites of national interest, under paragraph II, lett. f), provides that the settlement proposal «in the event of an involvement of several parties in causing the damage and of an obligation of reclamation, may be submitted even by only a few of them with regard to the entire obligation, without prejudice to the right of recourse towards the other parties involved».

---

[244] In this regard, the Constitutional Court expressed the historical judgment no. 364 of 1988, with reference to the interpretation of paragraph I of art. 27 of the Italian Constitution, according to which «criminal liability is personal».

[245] European Court of Justice, procedure C-534/13 of 2015.

[246] See also F. Degl'Innocenti, *Rischio d'impresa e responsabilità civile: la tutela dell'ambiente tra prevenzione e riparazione dei danni*, (Business Risk and civil liability: environmental protection between prevention and damage remediation), Firenze University Press, Florence 2013.

The aforementioned norm, rather than defining its scope of application with reference to Part Six of the Code, also involves the provisions concerning the reclamation of contaminated sites, as seen in Part Four.

Furthermore, the same provision seems to allow the implementation of the rules provided for by joint and several liability pursuant to art. 2055 of the Italian Civil Code, regardless of the ascertainment of the personal liability of the individual co-perpetrators of the damage to natural sites of national interest, which is instead provided for in art. 311, paragraph III, of the Code.

Lastly, a similar incompatibility can be found in art. 313, paragraph III according to which

with specific regard to compensation for damages, the ordinance is issued against the person liable for the damaging event as well as, jointly and severally, against the person in whose actual interest the conduct causing the damage was implemented or who objectively benefited from it by avoiding, as verified in the preliminary assessment, the economic burden necessary to carry out, as a preventive measure, the measures, equipment and precautions and to act as considered mandatory by the relevant norms.

The provision in question, therefore, attributes a solely negligent liability to the person obliged to compensate the environmental damage jointly with the operator in whose interest the conduct causing the damage was implemented, or who benefited from this conduct.

However, for him to be considered jointly liable, the operator must have failed to meet the required financial obligations necessary for the implementation of precautionary measures as well as to undertake actions to prevent the ecological damage, and this circumstance must be ascertained during the preliminary assessment.

The aforementioned form of negligent joint and several liability, therefore, on one hand does not consider the cases of strict liability for environmental damage caused by activities defined as dangerous under Part Six of the Code; on the other, it is in contrast with a re-affirmed and generic several liability in cases of involvement in the environmental damage event in itself, as per the last paragraph of art. 311, thus generating further problems for the systematic application of such legislation.

The systematics of the regulations on the prevention and remediation of environmental damage still present several critical points on a conceptual and technical level, thus raising considerable questions on the correct application of the legislation to the various cases.

The systematics of regulations regarding compensation for environmental damage still presents several critical points on a conceptual and technical level, thus raising considerable questions on the correct application of the legislation to the various cases.

The conceptual criticism focuses firstly on the meaning that was attributed to the environment.

This legal asset, specifically protected by European Directive 2004/35/EC and by Legislative Decree no. 152/2006 that implemented it, assumes a multitude of concepts and has a cross-cutting value.

The environment is first of all a system based on the interactions between all biotic and abiotic resources; secondly, it is a subjective right and at the same time a common interest, a material asset, even if cross-cutting.

With regard to the material and cross-cutting nature of the aforementioned asset, issues arise at the Italian constitutional level on the attribution of powers to the State for environmental protection and to the Regions for the exploitation of cultural and environmental assets, as established by art. 117 of the Italian Constitution.

The provision, in fact, in addition to not legally classifying the environment, which was also explicitly included in the constitutional text only with the 2001 reform, does not even clearly define the meaning of environmental asset exploitation, a notion that does not match the legal concept of environment as a subject per se, with a specific, limited object.

In this regard, it would be better to return to conceiving the object of the legislation examined here as a unitary, intangible asset as well as a cross-cutting value, elevating it to a constitutional right-obligation, in order to guarantee both its protection by the State, also increasing the joint participation of the population, and the individual rights to a healthy environment.

Even the notion of environmental damage raises some perplexities. In terms of the European legal system, in fact, the common legislation in Member States establishes a detailed, but at the same time exclusive, definition referring to standard assumptions and natural resources, determined, inter alia, with a distinction among them.

Within the special Italian legislation, a reversal was even implemented of the European provisions relating to the aforementioned notion since such notion first of all establishes an all-encompassing definition of damage to the environment similar to the European one that specifies the mere concept of damage; immediately after, however, damage to natural resources is described, exactly as in the framework directive.

Since supranational law and, in particular, the Italian law agree in considering the environment as a unitary ecological system, there should be no impediment to a precise, uniform re-elaboration of the notion of environmental damage, being this the only way to guarantee a uniform and overall protection of this asset.

With regard to formal and technical problems, various provisions of the Environmental Code contain typographical errors, a lack of syntactic connections, and references to obsolete norms, that are easily detectable. Moreover, other provisions generate overlaps of different legislation in environmental matters.

Instead, with regard to technical-substantive issues, code regulations are referred to, that could raise doubts on the chargeability of the operator or person liable, on the existence of a dual environmental liability system, especially when multiple parties are liable, and on determining the ecological damage compensation.

In fact, many of these regulations still refer to remedying damages in terms of monetary compensation, that is with an equivalent assets, contrary to what is provided for in the European Directive. In any case, in addition to specifically reintegrating the ecological damage in itself, no bans and injunction sanctions are foreseen, with the exception of temporary measures.

To this should be added a lack of provisions aimed at guaranteeing the prevention and remediation of environmental damages or the threat of them, even in cases where the operator is not identified or has to take action to prevent or remedy the damage.

In this regard, the State or competent authorities are not required to implement the aforementioned actions, nor is the operator obliged to have adequate insurance cover, even if he carries out a professional activity that is dangerous for health or the environment, as defined in the environmental legislation itself.

However, the European legislation expressly allows Member States to approve stricter rules to prevent and remedy environmental damage, which may also extend environmental liability to other parties in addition to the operator.

As a consequence, the national legislator is entitled to integrate preventive and compensatory protection against environmental damage, through provisions that include measures of a different and more rigorous nature, and extend environmental liability also towards the State in whose territory the ecological damage occurred.

Furthermore, the increase of a mandatory financial guarantee is allowed, by imposing operators to be insured also for damages deriving from the implementation of activities that are defined potentially dangerous for health and the environment.

It is also necessary to consider that the prospect of adopting stricter rules, not containing appropriate measures to reward virtuous operators or incentives for environment-friendly development, risks favoring the relocation of many activities of environmental importance towards Member States that endorse less strict and more useful regulations for operators.

Furthermore, ecological damage often spreads beyond national and

European borders where conflicts on the jurisdiction of States may occur also regarding the implementation of the relevant national regulations.

Only by reforming European legislation, therefore, or possibly even before that, by approving the hoped for International Environmental Code, will it be possible to avoid the aforesaid risk and ensure a uniform improvement of the legislation on environmental liability.

Therefore, a legislative action at different levels is reasonably deemed to be appropriate, that would confer a better systematic nature to the legislation as well as certainty in the implementation of an adequate preventive and compensatory protection to the environment, whose problems appear to be increasing and unstoppable due to the lack of sensitivity and to the superficiality with which they are approached by men.

ACERBONI F., *Contributo allo studio del principio di precauzione: dall'origine nel diritto internazionale a principio generale dell'ordinamento*, in Dir. Reg., 2000.

ALPA G., BESSONE M., *La responsabilità civile*, Giuffrè, 2001.

ALPA G., GAROFOLI R., *Manuale di diritto civile*, Nel Diritto Editore, 2015.

ANASTASI F., *La gestione dei siti inquinati: la responsabilità dell'inquinamento nella sentenza del TAR Lombardia n. 1326/2017*, in Riv. Giur. Lexambiente, July 20, 2017.

ASPRELLA C., *L'art. 96, comma 3, c.p.c tra danni punitivi e funzione indennitaria*, in Corr. Giur., 2016.

BIANCA C. M., *Diritto civile. V. La responsabilità*, Milan 2012.

BIGLIAZZI GERI L., *A proposito di danno ambientale ex art. 18 L. 8 July 1986, n. 349 e di responsabilità civile*, in Politica del diritto, 1987, p. 257.

BOSCOLO F., *Il risarcimento del danno ambientale. Profili di analisi*, CLEUP, 2015.

CAMONITA S., *La responsabilità di cose in custodia*, in Filodiritto, February 4, 2012.

CARINGELLA F., *Compendio di diritto amministrativo*, Dike giuridica, 2016.

CARTABIA M., LUPO N., SIMONCINI A., *Democracy and subsidiarity in the EU. National Parliaments, regions and civil society in the decision–making process*, in Percorsi, il Mulino, 2013.

CATENACCI M., *L'introduzione dei delitti contro l'ambiente nel codice penale. Una riforma con poche luci e molte ombre*, in Rivista quadrimestrale di diritto dell'ambiente, n. 2, 2015.

CAVANNA V., QUARANTA A., *La nuova transazione ambientale: il legislatore spariglia le carte?*, in Ambiente & sviluppo, n. 4/2016.

CECCHETTI M., *La materia "tutela dell'ambiente e dell'ecosistema" nella giurisprudenza costituzionale: lo stato dell'arte e i nodi ancora irrisolti*, in federalismi.it, Number 7–08/04/2009.

———, *Principi costituzionali per la tutela dell'ambiente*, Milan 2000.

CLARKE C., *La proposta della direttiva CE sulla responsabilità: a metà strada attraverso la procedura di codecisione*, in RECIEL, 2003.

DADDI T., *La prevenzione integrata dell'inquinamento e la gestione ambientale d'impresa. Applicazione della direttiva IPPC/IED ed effetti sulle imprese*, FrancoAngeli, 2014.

DEGL'INNOCENTI F., *Rischio d'impresa e responsabilità civile: la tutela dell'ambiente tra prevenzione e riparazione dei danni*, Firenze University Press, Florence 2013.

DESCOLA P., *L'ecologia degli altri. L'antropologia e la questione della natura*, Linaria, 2013.

DI GIACOMO RUSSO B., *Il valore della sussidiarietà. Origini e attualità*, in Dottrine e istituzioni, Città Nuova, 2015.

FOGLEMAN V., *La direttiva sulla responsabilità ambientale*, Env. L., 2004.

FRACCHIA F., *La tutela dell'ambiente come dovere di solidarietà*, in Diritto dell'economia, Enrico Mucchi, Modena 2009.

GARGALLO DI CASTEL LENTINI F., *L'ambiente come diritto fondamentale dell'uomo*, in www.dirittoambiente.com.

GIAMPIETRO F., *La Direttiva n. 2004/35/CE sulla responsabilità per danno all'ambiente messa a confronto con l'esperienza italiana*, Ambiente, 10, 2004.

GIANPIETRO P., *Prevenzione e riparazione del danno ambientale: la nuova direttiva n. 2004/35/CE*, Ambiente, 10, 2004.

GRAD P., *A legislative History of the Comprehensive Environmental Response, Compensation and Liability ("Superfund") Act of 1980*, 8 Colum. J. Env. L., 1, 1982.

GRASSI S., *Problemi di diritto costituzionale dell'ambiente*, Milan 2012.

GRONDONA M., *L'auspicabile "via libera" ai danni punitivi, il dubbio limite dell'ordine pubblico e la politica del diritto di matrice giurisprudenziale (a proposito del dialogo tra ordinamenti e giurisdizioni)*, in Dir. civ. cont., July 31, 2016.

HAFFNER P., *Visione cristiana dell'ambiente frutto della creazione di Dio*, Gracewing, 2012.

INZAGHI P., SERRATO R., *Se il proprietario è incolpevole non deve bonificare*, in Sviluppo e Territorio, November 18, 2015.

LUCARELLI F., *Ambiente, territorio e beni culturali nella giurisprudenza costituzionale*, Edizioni Scientifiche Italiane, 2006.

MAC AYEAL J. R., *The Comprehensive Environmental Response, Compensation, and Liability Act: The correct Paradigm of Strict Liability and the Problem of Individual Causation*, UCLA J. Env. L. & Pol., 2000.

MANCINI PALAMONI G., *Il principio di prevenzione*, in AmbienteDiritto.it, ISSN 1974–9562, November 26, 2014.

MARCATAJO G., *Il danno ambientale esistenziale*, Edizioni Scientifiche Italiane, 2016.

MICCICHÈ R., *Nuova direttiva europea in materia di responsabilità ambientale*, RGA, 2003.

MONTANARI T., *Costituzione incompiuta. Arte, paesaggio, ambiente*, Einaudi, 2013.

MUNARI F., SCHIANO DI PEPE L., *Responsabilità per gli illeciti ambientali in Europa: scelta del foro, scelta della legge e il caso per il perseguimento efficace dell'uniformità legale*, in RDIPP, 2005.

MUSELLA M., *La sussidiarietà orizzontale. Economia, politica, esperienze territoriali in Campania*, Carocci, 2012.

NIVARRA L., *Brevi considerazioni a margine dell'ordinanza di remissione alle Sezioni Unite sui "danni punitivi"*, in Dir. civ. cont. January 30, 2017.

PALLARO P., *Il principio di precauzione tra mercato interno e commercio internazionale: un'analisi del suo ruolo e del suo contenuto nel diritto comunitario*, in Dir. Comm. Internaz., 2002.

PAPA FRANCESCO, *Laudato si'. Testo integrale dell'enciclica*, curated by C. Simonelli, Piemme, 2015.

PATTI S., *Valori costituzionali e tutela dell'ambiente*, in G. Alpa e M. Alberighi, *Diritto e ambiente. Materiali di dottrina e giurisprudenza*, Padova 1984.

POLI S., *La responsabilità per danni da inquinamento transfrontaliero nel diritto comunitario e internazionale*, Milan 2006.

POLITI M., *Tutela dell'ambiente e «sviluppo sostenibile». Profili e prospettive di evoluzione nel diritto internazionale alla luce della Conferenza di Rio de Janeiro*, Padova 1995.

PORENA D., *La protezione dell'ambiente tra Costituzione italiana e "Costituzione globale"*, Giappichelli, Turin 2009.

POTTIER A., *Comment les économistes réchauffent la planète*, SEUIL, 2016.

POZZO B., *La proposta di nuova direttiva sulla prevenzione e il risarcimento del danno all'ambiente,* Danno e Resp., 2002.

————, *La nuova Direttiva 2004/35 del Parlamento europeo e del Consiglio sulla responsabilità in materia di prevenzione e riparazione del danno*, RGA, 1, 2006.

POZZO B., RENNA M., *L'ambiente nel nuovo titolo V della Costituzione*, Giuffrè, 2004.

PRATI L., *Responsabilità per danno all'ambiente e bonifica dei siti contaminati*, IPSOA Gruppo Wolters Kluwer, Milanofiori Assago (MI) 2011.

RODOTÀ S., *Il problema della responsabilità civile*, Milan 1964.

SACHS J. D., *L'era dello sviluppo sostenibile*, in Frontiere, Università Bocconi Editore, 2015.

SALVIA F., *Ambiente e sviluppo sostenibile*, in Rivista Giuridica Ambiente, 1998.

SCARSELLI, *Il nuovo art. 96, 3° comma, c.p.c.: consigli per l'uso*, in Foro it., 2010.

SCHIRIPPA M., *I danni punitivi nel panorama internazionale e nella situazione italiana: verso il loro riconoscimento?*, in www.comparazionedirittocivile.it, March 2017.

STERN SWITZER C., BULAN L. A., *CERCLA: Comprehensive Environmental Response, Compensation and Liability Act (superfund)*, Section of Environment, Energy, and Resources Book Publications Committee, 2002.

TRIMARCHI P., *Rischio e responsabilità oggettiva*, Milan 1961.

ZILIOLI C., *L'applicazione del principio di sussidiarietà nel diritto comunitario dell'ambiente*, in Rivista Giuridica Ambiente, 1995.

Youcanprint
Finito di stampare nel mese di giugno 2019